Acclaim for Bree Sullivan Crush Your Divorce & Keep Your Faith

Yahoo! Finance: "Sullivan-Howell uses scripture to encourage, not shame, women going through the trauma of divorce. She guides them to build spiritual, emotional and financial stability throughout the process. Her legal expertise helps demystify navigating complex divorce proceedings as a woman of faith."

"With a mission to reconnect with the promises of God's Word to give hope and comfort, *Crush Your Divorce® & Keep Your Faith* author and attorney Bree Sullivan-Howell shares experiences and lessons learned from over two decades as a leading divorce attorney, along with insights from her own divorce journey."

Fox: "*Crush Your Divorce®* offers practical solutions centered on biblical truth and grace for women navigating marital dissolution."

"Women need compassion and empowerment during chaotic marital dissolution. Sullivan-Howell is helping fill this gap through her unique work supporting Christian women navigating divorce. She offers faith-based services for those facing divorce all the way through rebuilding life after the divorce is finalized. Her book and online resources remove the veil of silence and stigma."

"*Crush Your Divorce®* aims to teach why it's not unladylike or unChristian to stand up for yourself, as well as help people gain valuable, practical insight into the nuts and bolts of a divorce case—including strategies on how to help your lawyer prepare your case to win."

ABC: "*Crush Your Divorce®* helps Christian women find their voice during a divorce, especially those experiencing abandonment or abuse."

NBC: "Sullivan-Howell's message offers a path forward, bringing God's light into the darkness of divorce and empowering women to crush its hold over their lives. There is hope, healing and wholeness after divorce ends a Christian marriage. Sullivan-Howell is helping lead the way."

CRUSH
YOUR
COMEBACK

CRUSH YOUR COMEBACK

Bree Sullivan-Howell, J.D.

PALMETTO
PUBLISHING
Charleston, SC
www.PalmettoPublishing.com

Copyright © 2023 by Crush Your Divorce, LLC

All rights reserved

No portion of this book may be reproduced, stored in a retrieval system, or transmitted in any form by any means–electronic, mechanical, photocopy, recording, or other–except for brief quotations in printed reviews, without prior permission of the author.

Cover art: Sharon Heard
Headshot: Ursula Page Photography

Hardcover ISBN: 979-8-8229-3576-1
Paperback ISBN: 979-8-8229-3577-8
eBook ISBN: 979-8-8229-3578-5

Dedication

*For every woman who's found the gumption to keep breathing,
believing and walking forward when her heart was shattered,
and her world was suddenly scary and uncertain.
You are the brave ones.*

Table of Contents

Introduction xiii

1. Let Yourself Go 1
   Let Yourself Go and Do All the Things
   Your Ex Would Never Allow 1
   Let Yourself Go and Serve Others 2
   He's Doing a Mighty Work in You 3
2. Create a New Space 6
   Make Happy New Memories in the Same Places You've Cried 7
3. Craft Your Comeback 9
   Consider the Proverbs 31 Woman 10
   Mia's Story 11
   Let's Be Clear: You Need a New Financial Plan,
   Not a New Man 14
   You've Got This 16
4. Make a New Estate Plan 28
   Last Will and Testament 28
   Health Care Directives and Financial Agents 29
   Consider a Trust 29
   Plan for College 30
5. Dads are Important 32
6. Coparenting and Counterparenting:
   Architecture, Not Archeology 38
   Good Coparents are Architects 38
   Lose the Archeology Mindset 39
   Respectful Communication and
   Appropriate Boundaries are Key 41

    Coparenting with a Crazy Person 42

    Pollyanna's Story 43

    If Your Ex is a Quarrelsome Coparent 47

    Try Parallel Parenting 49

    Supporting Children through High-Conflict Coparenting 49

7. Get Your Groove Back: Modern Dating 55

    The Lost Years Will be Restored to You 55

    You Don't *Need* a Man to be Happy. 55

    Heal and Don't Look Back 57

    You Are Not Too Old, and It Is Not Too Late 59

    Guard Your Heart and Mind Your Soul Ties 60

    What Kind of Guy Should I Look For? 60

    Red Flags to Avoid. 63

    Don't Be Afraid to Give New Love a Chance 65

    Your Ex and Kids Could Try to Ruin It 67

    Don't Make It Public Until You Know It's Permanent 68

    Marin's Story 68

8. Graceful Family Blending 73

    Blended Families are Special 73

    Stepparenting. 74

    Introducing a New Stepparent 76

    How a Prenuptial Agreement Can

    Keep Your Next Marriage Together. 78

9. There's Hope for Us All 82

    Acknowledgments. 87

    About the Author 91

    Let's connect! 92

Author's Note

I carved this book out of *Crush Your Divorce & Keep Your Faith* when the editors told me I'd written too much for it all to be one work. I apparently had more to say than I'd initially thought. ☺ I pray that both books, taken together, provide a solid roadmap for your walk through Divorceland and also the Wonderland beyond. This book was originally Part Four of *Crush Your Divorce*, and it's all about hope and logistics for your post-divorce life after the litigation is done. It's a good idea to read both books together.

The stories in this book and people named herein are <u>PURELY HYPOTHETICAL</u> composite characters based on general themes drawn from the multidimensional experiences of those close to me, random case studies I've researched, fact patterns from publicly available case law, and online divorce survivor blogs I've studied over the years. These stories are here to let you know you are not alone, to show you the importance of perseverance and to demonstrate that joy is possible on the other side of this challenging time. They are not any particular person's story, and all names are <u>purely fictitious</u>. Don't even try to guess who I might be talking about in each hypothetical, as they are <u>not real people</u>.

<u>BIG Disclaimer</u>: Nothing in the book should be construed as legal advice for your particular situation. Laws differ from state to state. You MUST seek your own attorney in your jurisdiction for individualized guidance tailored to address the particular issues of your unique story. While I hope my words give you food for thought and help you frame questions for your lawyer, and I'm thankful you're interested in my insight, *I cannot advise you, and I do not represent you in your case just because you picked up my book.*

There is a Resource section at the end of each chapter to give you other helpful things to read and listen to along your divorce journey. There is so much wisdom out there, and we should never stop learning and growing! Questions for Reflection are likewise included at the end of each chapter for you to consider during your quiet time and in group study with your friends and supporters.

I've also included a soundtrack of tunes pertinent to the struggles explored in each chapter, as music can be such a great source of comfort. I pray it will be a balm on your sweet, shattered heart, empower you and lighten your mood as you wrestle with your situation and begin to heal. Check out my "Crush Your Divorce | Keep Your Faith" and "Soundtrack for the Divorcing" playlists on Spotify.

I'm praying for you, Dear Reader, to be strengthened and encouraged to look forward to the new day to come after your divorce is over. I pray boldly for God to work mightily in your life, draw you close, and be glorified in your story. Divorce or no divorce, your relationship with Him is the most important thing you have. May you praise Him in your storm and also in your victories.

xo, BSH

Introduction

Jabez cried out to the God of Israel, "Oh, that you would bless me and enlarge my territory! Let your hand be with me, and keep me from harm so that I will be free from pain." And God granted his request . . . (1 Chronicles 4:10).

Are you old enough to remember when *The Prayer of Jabez* was released? My mother bought me a copy of this powerful little book when I was in law school. It seemed like references to Jabez and his prayer were everywhere back then! Everyone was praying that God would "bless them, indeed," and enlarge their territory for the kingdom. I loved it then, and I still love it now.

Jabez's prayer was bold as he prayed in faithful expectation that God would surely bless him and expand his reach for the Lord, but it was also a very simple prayer of humility as he expectantly asked that "God's hand be with him." Jabez surely wanted to be blessed, to be free from harm and pain, and to do good in the world in obedience to the Lord, but more than that he wanted to be on God's team. I believe this is all any of us really want out of life, but I wonder how often we're willing to bring our requests to the Lord in honest expectation that He will honor them. I love how Jabez just boldly brings his desires straight to God.

We can pray the same way, Friend. When you talk to God about the longings of your heart, it doesn't have to be fancy to be effective. God honored Jabez's request because he came to the throne with the right motives . . . to be shielded from evil, to be used by God in a mighty, extensive way. It's my prayer for you today that God will show you His good plan for your life and expand your reach for His glory—both in your business and career ventures and in your personal relationships.

One of the best things about divorce is that your budget becomes your own, to prioritize and allocate as you wish. It can almost feel like a pay raise when you get to stop supporting Mr. Used-to-be-Wonderful's hobbies and habits! As a divorced woman, you will have the freedom to broaden your reach to do good in the world by donating to causes you love, things your husband never allowed you to support when you were married. You'll also be free to tithe your funds, which is especially liberating for those ladies whose husbands forbade giving to the church during the marriage.

Perhaps the most priceless way to multiply the good you're putting into the world is to raise your children well, in a home full of love and hospitality. Part of building back better is the blessing to parent in peace in your home without your ex undermining your every parenting decision. Build your new life with the creation of new traditions and fun, unforgettable experiences. Host all those friends and family members your ex never allowed you to have over, feather your nest with the flowers and candles you need to make your guests feel honored (the things you were never allowed to buy when you were married), cook what you want to serve, give the gifts you want people to have, be the loving woman you want to be.

Ecclesiastes 3:17 tells us everything has a season, and every time of your life has a purpose. This post-divorce season is a precious and sacred time for you to get with God and embrace His renewed purpose for your life.

This little book is to get you in the mindset of fostering growth—spiritual, relational, professional, financial and personal—after your marriage has ended. Life is tremendous and full of adventure! Now's the time to leave the ashes behind and build something beautiful! May it be a life you love.

1

Let Yourself Go

"There are far, far better things ahead than any we leave behind."
—C.S. Lewis

When your divorce is over, it's time to let yourself go. No, I don't mean you should eat a daily gallon of Blue Bell, become a pothead or drink yourself into oblivion. What I mean is that your time of mourning is over, and now it's the season to dance! This is YOUR time, Dear One! Your moment to decide whether you're going to let this divorce break you and change you for the worse, or if you'll overcome the sadness and grab life with both hands.

Let Yourself Go and Do All the Things Your Ex Would Never Allow

While my divorce was still underway, I went ahead and planned some exciting things to look forward to. They were all things I never would have been comfortable doing during my first marriage. There was a week in England with my besties (my first trip overseas)—AMAZING! Tickets to not one but *two* John Mayer shows, and the second one in Aspen, miraculously, turned out to be part of my second honeymoon—a FULL CIRCLE MOMENT! I booked an art night for my paralegals and me, and we left there with fresh artwork for our homes—LIFE-GIVING! Some friends and I started a Sunday afternoon walking group—ENRICHING GIRL TIME! I saved up for the luggage set I'd always wanted but had been afraid to buy, reconnected with friends from long ago, and started hosting parties for my side of the family—A NEW DAY! Others I know have trained for triathlons, become real estate agents, gone back to school, and myriad other remarkable things after their divorces. You're next!

Let Yourself Go and Serve Others

Martin Luther King, Jr. said, "Everybody can be great... because anybody can serve. You don't have to have a college degree to serve. You don't have to make your subject and verb agree to serve. You only need a heart full of grace. A soul generated by love."

Consider the admonition of Ephesians 5:14-17 that we <u>redeem the time</u> we're given. How can you get started redeeming the time you have left on this earth? How can you fulfill your purpose to glorify God in the time you have left?

Life goes on after your divorce, and this world is not all about you. The more you're able to shift your focus from your own pain and concentrate on how to better the lives of your fellow humans, the further removed from you that pain will be. As you look to meet the needs of those around you, you'll get outside yourself, start to forget your own problems and begin to feel a growing sense of accomplishment with each person you touch. Bloom where you're planted in this season, Dear One, and ask God to use you where He might.

Remember how Forrest Gump got to safety, and then ran back into the Vietnamese jungle to rescue his friends? Once you've healed from this divorce and can see others struggling with the same things, you have an obligation to run into the chaos and help someone just like you. Serve the woman you once were.

He's Doing a Mighty Work in You

Perhaps you have regrets about your past that make you feel unworthy to serve or help anyone else. When you feel this way, remember Jesus' interaction with the woman at the well. She had been divorced five times, and Jesus still used her. A complicated past does not disqualify you from service to others. If anything, it makes you more relatable to the very people who need to hear from you the most! God sees your potential even when you cannot.

When I was a little girl, I would sit on the floor next to my mom as she worked on her cross-stitch projects. From my place at her feet, I would look up at the back of her craft to see the design-less bunch of different-colored threads. From that vantage point below, you could never guess the beauty of the art being created on top. When finished and framed into a wall hanging, pillow front or Christmas ornament, you didn't see the backside of the work, just the lovely, seamless design of a flower, animal or fleur-de-lis on the front. What looked from below like a disorderly waste of time was working together to make something magnificent for the world to enjoy.

Dear Friend, we serve a God of order who brings symmetry and organization to our messy lives. Your life is like that tangled bunch of thread in my mama's cross-stitching. You can't imagine how anything useful—let alone beautiful—could ever come out of it. But God sees that top part—our true potential, our true wonder as His creation—from a bird's eye view. He knows that your hidden mess will be an exquisite work of art when it's completed. Oh, praise Him for blessing our messes!

Questions for Reflection

1. Think of a time in your life when you felt most alive and most at peace with yourself. How were you spending your time? With *whom* were you spending your time?
2. What wanderlust or thirst for adventure is stirring in your heart? How can you make those things happen in real life?
3. What needs do you see in the community around you? Are there volunteer or community activities which would fit with your skill set and heart for service? Consider opportunities to serve in light of Galatians 6:9.
4. Consider Romans 12:9's admonishment: "Don't just pretend that you love others: really love them." How can you use your gifts to love others well? Who do you know that needs your unique encouragement and support?
5. Think of yourself as God's handiwork. What storms has He brought you through that have strengthened you for ministry to others? What is He preparing you to do in your post-divorce life for His kingdom? What can you start doing today so that you'll be proud of the life you built, when you look back twenty years from now?

Resources

Eat, Pray, Love—Elizabeth Gilbert (and the 2010 film with Julia Roberts)
Fun: 100 Days to Discover Fun Right Where You Are—Annie F. Downs
Redeeming the Time—Chuck D. Pierce
It's Never Too Late—Kathy Lee Gifford
Finding Meaning in the Second Half of Life—James Hollis
Halftime—Bob Buford

Chapter Soundtrack

"Wildflowers"—Tom Petty

"She Let Herself Go"—George Strait

"Turn! Turn! Turn!"—the Byrds

"Miss Me More"—Kelsea Ballerini

"Unanswered Prayers"—Garth Brooks

"Anyway"—Martina McBride

2

Create a New Space

"Home is the nicest word there is."
—Laura Ingalls Wilder

Women, by and large, love a feathered, clean, organized nest, and it can take years to get your home just like you want it. That's why so many divorcing women struggle with the changes in their home atmosphere when furniture and décor is divided or when relocating to a whole new location. The sooner you can create a new space for yourself post-separation, the better you're going to feel.

If you kept the marital home, it may look a little different if your ex took a chunk of the household furniture when he left. Do not let this stress you out. Instead, look at it as a chance to make your home setting something that reflects *your* personality. You can do it all your way this time around, without asking anyone's opinion! Liberating! If you can't afford new furniture, look on the Facebook Marketplace and other locations where secondhand items are sold for a bargain; it's amazing to see the quality items people give away in this throwaway culture of ours. You can also rearrange the furniture you have to bring a fresh feel to the place.

You should purge all items that remind you of your ex, if they bring you pain. The space must be revamped into a setting for *new, happy* memories to be made in what has been a place of sadness. One client reported that the jars of her husband's pickled peppers taunted her each time she saw them in the pantry. She felt better when she donated them to the local food bank. Problem solved. Identify these kinds of triggers for you and get them out of your space.

Whatever your decorating preference, the goal is to make the home reflect *your* personality and *your* style, incorporating those colors and fabrics that make *your* heart happy and *your* body most comfortable. It's amazing what the right home environment can do for your mental health.

You should also give your kids the creative license to update their own spaces in the home. As your budget will allow, let them pick new bedding, lamps, and paint colors, and enjoy painting and redoing their rooms together. Doing this does a few things. First, it makes a happy memory of this otherwise painful time of transition. Second, it assures them that you are committed to their comfort. Third, it gives your children a little bit of ownership in and authority over this post-divorce situation to which you're all trying to adjust. Your children's rooms are their safe havens, and you want them to be comfortable at your house. My kids all have photos of their dad in their rooms at my house, and I hope they have photos of me in their rooms at his house. Photos of the other parent can help ease the anxiety of separation by making the other parent feel closer to the child. Moreover, your act of placing these photos in a child's room is a silent signal to let the child know he's free to love your ex, and that you don't expect him to "pick a side."

Make Happy New Memories in the Same Places You've Cried

About four months after my divorce was final, thinking I needed a fresh start elsewhere, I listed my house for sale. I didn't want to live in a place with so many difficult memories. How thankful I am now that no one bought it! Today, my home has a whole new feel to it. As soon as my ex and his mama got their furniture from my house, the first thing I did was add loads of pillows, candles, pink accents and my mom's abstract paintings in every room, still keeping the furniture fairly minimal. Once all that old, brown, leather furniture was gone, I realized that less truly is *more*. It looks like the Barbie Dream House up in there! And adding new flower beds and hedges of glorious evergreen trees completely changed the exterior landscape, too. It's truly like a different house now because of all the new memories we've made. I praise the Lord that the same rooms I cried in before are now filled with peace, calm, fun and laughter. May it also be the same for you. ♥

Question for Reflection

Are you struggling with letting go of belongings acquired during your marriage, or struggling with putting your home back together after a divorce? Contemplate the words of Matthew 6:19 that caution us not to "store up for yourselves treasures on earth, where moths and vermin destroy, and where thieves break in and steal." What can this passage teach us about keeping our attachment to things in check?

Resources

The Joy of Decorating: Southern Style with Mrs. Howard—Phoebe Howard

She Made Herself a Home—Rachel Van Kluyve

Soundtrack

"Blessings"—Laura Story

"A New Day Has Come"—Celine Dion

"Here Comes the Sun"—the Beatles

"Cool Change"—Little River Band

"Time to Move On"—Tom Petty

"All I've Ever Known"—Alexandra Kay

3

Craft Your Comeback

*"I don't like to gamble, but if there is
one thing I'm willing to bet on, it's myself."*
—Beyoncé

Are you a young mother who gave up her career to raise the children? Your husband has left you, and you're afraid you won't make it?

I see you.

Are you a middle-aged woman whose children are older now but still need a lot of your time, wondering how you will start a new career after leaving an abusive, alcoholic husband? Are you an older woman whose children are grown and flown, whose husband has abruptly left you for another, perhaps younger, woman without advance warning, and you are desperately trying to figure out how you will manage the affairs of life without him and his income? You've been kept in the dark and never had to pay bills in your adult life, and not sure where to begin? He's left, or you've had to leave for your own well-being, just when you were supposed to start traveling and enjoying retirement together, and you're devastated and unsure of your next move toward financial freedom?

I see you. I've felt these same fears. This chapter is for you.

Consider the Proverbs 31 Woman

I have always aspired to be the woman of good character described in Proverbs 31. She's one really cool chick.

She serves her family and meets their daily needs, but she's also out there wheeling and dealing in real estate, "considering fields and buying them." She can handle her own financial affairs without her husband's help.

She's up late making stuff, probably to sell. The work of her hands is fruitful. She's no doubt making food, doing laundry, and keeping her home, but she's also out there making money and creating. She's a badass.

She's independent. Everyone else in the house is sleeping as she burns that midnight oil. In the quiet stillness of the night, she labors away quietly, diligently, blessing her household, asking for no recognition.

Like all our lives these days, her days are full of commitments, and she must be a very organized person, redeeming every minute, or else she couldn't accomplish all that she does. She's not a woman who would mindlessly scroll her Instagram feed or watch a lot of TV. No way. This Proverbs 31 woman makes the most of her time on earth.

She brings honor and glory to her Father in Heaven and makes her family proud.

She's the kind of woman I want to be. She's the kind of woman we should all aspire to be, whether we be single, married, divorced, remarried or widowed.

So how can you emulate this Proverbs 31 ideal as a freshly divorced woman?

Girl, get excited! The world is your oyster.

Mia's Story

Mia never thought she'd find herself divorced at fifty years old, but here she was.

She had a degree in accounting from a prestigious university and was working with a Big Four accounting firm with a bright future and a nice office in a fancy Atlanta skyscraper when Matthew came along. He was a young lawyer working with a well-respected firm in her same office building. They'd met one day in the basement cafeteria, both of them reaching for the same dessert, and the rest was history. Drawn to Mia's confidence, outgoing personality and warm sense of humor, Matthew assertively and persistently pursued Mia until she simply could not ward him off any longer. He swept her off her feet with his charming advances and asked her to marry him on her twenty-sixth birthday. While she wasn't sure it was true love like the kind you read about in novels, Mia (always the logical one) felt the relationship made a lot of sense, for Matthew was cute, successful and kind, the sort of guy any girl would want to build a life with. She accepted his proposal, and they were married the following year in a quiet ceremony at the Cloister on Sea Island.

Matthew was a good husband but had to work an awful lot. He made partner in his firm's mergers and acquisitions department after he and Mia had been married just three years, and with partnership came significant demands on his time. By then, they had little Micah, and they decided it made the most sense for Mia to leave her job to stay home with the baby because Matthew's earning potential was so much greater than hers, and they didn't want their children raised by nannies.

They took two vacations each year, one during the summer and the other at Christmastime, and Matthew had his laptop with him during both, never truly able to unplug and enjoy the family. Mia wished they could have more time together, but she told herself that all Matthew's hard work would *pay off one day, and he wouldn't have to work so much. Sadly, that day never came.*

Just after Micah started school, just as Mia was considering going back to work, along came Mimi, Baby Number Two, closely followed just 18 months later by Baby Number Three, Maxwell. The perfect family. Mia was content at home with the kids and, while she missed her career, she knew her calling to be a mother was more important for the season they were in.

Things went fine for a period of years, or so Mia thought. Matthew's work took him out of town and regularly required late nights at the office, but he was an attentive dad when he was home. She never would have guessed he had fallen in love with his paralegal.

The revelation of Matthew's years-long affair with the woman in his office cut Mia to her core. How could he love this woman? She was, after all, no Mia. Mia wrestled with how this could have happened, to understand why they were no longer the epic couple they once had been. After much analysis and many therapy sessions, Mia deduced that they'd probably been doomed from the moment she gave up her job. When she did that, she'd lost her independence, her intrigue. Matthew wasn't as attracted to this "mothering" version of Mia, as dreadful as it was to admit. Matthew had just lost interest in her. And, if she was being honest, she had never been all that interested in him, either; she'd elected the rational choice in life partners rather than holding out for real, genuine, knock-you-off-your-feet, hit-you-in-the-face, undeniable, true love. She knew she was as much to blame for this growing apart as he was.

So, survivor that she was, Mia made herself stop crying about the demise of her marriage in short order. She'd always been good with numbers and was a natural master at making sense of data. Instead of allowing herself to wallow in self-pity and sadness over the demise of her precious family, she opted instead to accept the challenge to overcome and make something awesome from this heartbreaking circumstance. She would not let him (or Paralegal

Tiffany) break her. She would overcome her circumstances and show her kids how a woman should handle this sort of adversity—with grace, poise and laser focus.

When Matthew hired the meanest divorce lawyer in town and tried to make the divorce all her fault, Mia took the gloves off. Instead of just owning his mistake and endeavoring to make it right with a fair settlement, Matthew allowed his lawyer to create a narrative that Mia had been a spendthrift and had sexually neglected him. None of that was true.

He ran up new credit card debts while the divorce case was pending, all to try to look poor to the court and avoid paying Mia the alimony and division of property he rightfully should pay. He spent freely while limiting Mia's access to money, questioning every purchase she made when he'd never cared before. Mia knew she was in this vulnerable position because she'd given up her employment years prior; otherwise, she wouldn't be so reliant on Matthew for her very survival. And she didn't like this feeling of dependence at all—not one little bit. She vowed she'd never be in such a position ever again.

When Matthew filed for divorce, Mia sent resumes to all her old contacts in the accounting world and was able to secure a job at her old firm. She'd have to work her way back into the office culture, as a lot had changed in the years she'd been away, but she knew she could do it, and she loved that kind of work anyway, so it didn't feel like work to her. The kids were older and no longer needed her to be in the home all the time, so the new position she'd been offered would be perfect.

Following the divorce, Mia was able to work her way back up the corporate ladder and earn a substantial income as a CPA and auditor. She loved the clients, the office culture and meeting new people. She enrolled in an online college program and received additional credentials in financial planning so that she could help other women like her rebuild and plan their financial futures after divorce. She began to save money and got into real estate investing,

investing small down payments into properties her tenants finished paying off for her with their monthly rent. She even rented out the garage apartment at her home and used the money to pay her mortgage! She studied the stock market and found an exceptional financial advisor to help her with diversifying her investments.

By investing her money wisely, Mia became financially free, without any fear of how she would support herself in retirement. And, eventually, when she least expected it, she found new love like she'd never known.

Let's Be Clear: You Need a New Financial Plan, Not a New Man

I once had a client who'd divorced her husband in the 1980s and gotten a lifetime alimony award, complete with annual cost-of-living adjustments and all her health costs paid in full through the time of her death. This lady was having her ex-husband pay for her dental implants well into her eighties! She got in on the tail-end of the days of lifetime alimony awards; they are now a thing of the past. The women's liberation movement and its resulting widespread employment and empowerment of women changed everything for divorcing women nationwide. Praise Jesus, women now have the legal rights they fought so hard for—the right to be paid the same as men, the right to be considered for positions based on abilities and qualifications, unhindered by traditional gender roles. As a result, our judges, juries and populace now expect women to pick themselves up after a divorce and become self-supporting, at least to a large degree. This revolution, while it's been amazing for the working women of our country, is a shock to those women who don't work outside the home who find themselves in divorces and in need of sustainable income sources apart from their ex-husbands.

Are you afraid of how you will afford your living expenses, post-divorce? If so, you're not alone. In one survey, thirty-seven percent of married women said that they would *not* stay married if they were not financially dependent on their husbands. That's a lot of women trapped in marriages by financial insecurity, and not afraid to admit it! And I surmise the true percentage is even higher than that.

This is your chance to dig deep. To figure out how you will make it without your ex. To spread your wings and soar! Get excited!

You are wise to analyze what your finances will look like after Mr. Used-to-be-Wonderful is out of the picture. You are no longer going to have the full benefit of your husband's income, and you are now going to be the single person in charge of funding your household's needs.

Sister, a new man is not a financial plan.[1] You got free of the last one, so let's not go tying our security and net worth to a new one just yet, okay? It's a terrible thing to be beholden to a man for your very survival, to have to remarry before you're ready or move in with a man just to survive. Avoid this at all costs! Being financially secure broadens your options and keeps you from forcing the *wrong* relationship to fruition. The imbalance of financial power in a relationship can create issues from the jump.

A woman who knows her worth doesn't chase a new man for his money. Read that again.

Before diving into a new, financially dependent relationship, it's better to get yourself together first. And when you do, the men will flock to you, assuming you even want them to.

Never settle your case on the assumption that you will just find another husband right away to be your financial support. You may be single for a while, and a period of singleness may be needed before you're emotionally ready for a new beau. Even if you are leaving your

---

[1] Quote by Mary Waring. See *https://www.thedivorcemagazine.co.uk/mary-waring/*

spouse because you have already fallen in love with someone else, that relationship could also fail. Just being honest—if you started the relationship in adultery, there is a higher likelihood that you or your new spouse will cheat on one another someday is real. Don't set yourself up to be twice-divorced *and* poor. Plus, it's the opposite of romantic to feel forced to marry someone to survive. Relationships are most enriching, I've learned, when both partners independently bring something interesting and valuable to them. Financial freedom gives you a lot of options in your dating life, right down to the choice of whether to date at all! So many women—myself included—were/are just fine living single immediately after they divorce.

You've Got This

I left my marriage with my home, my office and what's cooking in my brain, but very little money in the bank, taxes due and a whopping mortgage to pay by myself. Talk about a step out in faith! I prayed every day and had to trust God to keep me healthy enough to work, as I knew that was the key to getting back on firm financial footing. It was such a raw, vulnerable, precious time with the Lord. And He was so very, very faithful to put me back on stable ground after my world imploded.

You may be thinking, "but you had an established career when you divorced, and I've never worked outside the home! What about me?" It's a fair point, but even if you've not worked outside the home in a minute, take heart! Managing the household's daily affairs and schedules have certainly prepared you to juggle all the balls, multitask, organize, and prioritize tasks. . . all skills which are needed to make money, too! Women who manage households are pure dynamite in the business world.

Here are Ten Big Ideas to keep in mind as you regroup:

1. **Analyze your budget, and plan for variable expenses.** Ask your lawyer or the paralegal on your case to help you analyze your budget. Are you spending too much on clothes and Starbucks? Are you going to have to pay certain bills after your divorce that your husband is paying now? You need to take all of this into account. The financial disclosure form we use in Georgia is useful in helping you consider all the categories of your spending and identify which items are top priorities and which can go. I suspect other states have similar financial disclosure forms to help you analyze your finances to figure out what you need each month to support your budget. Take the time to give it some careful thought early in your case, and make sure your attorney is clear on your needs before that first hearing. Whatever you end up getting in your divorce will be a starting point for all future financial planning.

    Health insurance premiums are a moving target and vary greatly from person to person, state to state. State marketplace exchanges can be difficult to maneuver, and you need to confirm you qualify before assuming cheap benefits are available to you. COBRA coverage is an option for some people which makes your existing coverage available to you for a period of months following your divorce, but COBRA premiums can be much higher than what you paid when you were married. Make sure you know what you're getting into before you finalize the terms of your divorce.

    Utilities costs vary with the seasons and can stress your budget if you don't plan for them. In South Georgia, our summer power bills are through the roof as we pump cold air into our houses, and I suspect the same is true for those of you up north as you heat your homes in the wintertime. As you're planning your post-divorce budget, it's a good idea to study a calendar year's worth of utility bills to determine what you should expect to pay, month to month.

2. **Get all you can from Mr. Used-to-be-Wonderful.** Your lawyer can help you get a solid settlement or judgment in your case to start your singledom off on firm footing. Carefully analyze which items in your marital estate have lasting value and are likely to appreciate in the future, and seek those items in your settlement or trial. If you have income-producing rental property, for instance, you should consider asking for them; you can find help to manage it, and the income it creates could give you substantial buying power well into your retirement years. You may also want to seek a recovery of alimony, or even a court order requiring your spouse to pay your education costs as needed for you to obtain adequate employment. I go into this topic more fully in my chapter on alimony and child support in *Crush Your Divorce & Keep Your Faith* if you'd like to dive in a little deeper.

3. **Consider hiring a financial planner.** Did your husband take care of all your financial matters such that now you know very little about what you have or even what some things cost? Or did he even outright deny you a seat at the table whenever discussions of investment strategy, interest rates, bond yields, dividends and market trends were discussed? If so, and especially if you received assets in your divorce which you must now invest somehow, you may want to consider consulting with a certified financial planner for help in deciding how to manage expenses and allocate your investments.

Gold brokers will try to sell you gold. Cryptocurrency traders will tell you crypto is the investment of the future. Stock portfolio managers will tell you your money is safest in stocks. Life insurance guys want to buy their policies and annuities. Realtors sell real estate. Art dealers tout the wonders of art investing. My point is that everyone has a plausible argument for why you should put your money in whatever they're selling, and they can't all be right, at least not all at the same time. I'm not a financial planning expert, which is why I refer my clients to people who are.

I've represented countless women in this situation at the end of their divorce cases. They suddenly have all these assets to invest and fear they'll make the wrong move. If this is your situation, what you need is a licensed Certified Divorce Financial Planner (CDFP) to look at your entire portfolio and advise you on how to allocate your resources to maximize your financial security for the future; even more valuable is the CDFP's alimony analysis and tax-saving/tax-avoidance advice as you consider various settlement scenarios. A person has to go through a ton of training and pass a difficult test in order to become a CDFP. My clients will tell you a CDFP is worth every nickel you pay them. Check the resources below to find a CDFP in your area.

If you can't afford a CDFP or don't have enough assets to justify the costs of a CDFP, check out Savvy Ladies at www.savvyladies.org for some outstanding (and free) financial education resources tailored to the needs and concerns of divorcing women. The site offers webinars, and there's even a hotline you can call with questions.

4. **Get yourself a mentor**. Find a woman who has been through a divorce and came out financially secure and happy on the other side, and make that woman your mentor. She is a wealth of knowledge and your best asset. Let her help you avoid mistakes. And one day, when you're through these woods, you will mentor someone else with your mentor's wisdom as your example. Older women helping the younger women, carrying all that kindness forward, just like we're told to do in Titus 2:4-8. I love it! There is strength when we come together and help one another. Isn't it beautiful how God gives us the people we need, when we need them? God gets us out of our pits so that we can go back in and get others out!

5. **Identify and build on your strengths**. No sense trying to force a round peg into a square hole. Your employment future will likely be much more sustainable if you chart a new course based on something you've already got a knack for. Do you love children? Keeping your own children anyway? Consider watching your friend's children and be their day care provider. Are you an artist? Look for ways to sell your art online, and promote yourself on social media, free of charge. People will pay good money for the unique things you make. Are you good with people? Look into a job in sales or marketing! Companies are always looking for personable sales reps, and they'll train you to do the job. Sales jobs are also great ways to meet new, interesting people and get yourself out of the funk you may be in because of your divorce. Are you good with interior design? Start a design service! The idea is to identify what you're good at, and hone that skill until it's a moneymaker.

6. **Build on your background**. What did you study in school? What skills do you have from on-the-job training or education? It's often easier to build your resume from where you last left off than to start over with a new career entirely. You may have to obtain recertification or a new license, but resuming an old career path is usually the easiest choice. Check with your former colleagues and consult your alma mater's career placement office for resources and guidance about opportunities to explore.

7. **Consider real estate**. Just a century ago, women weren't allowed to open a bank account or own property. But now, thirty percent of American real estate investors—including me—are women. There are many ways to get into the real estate game. Are you gifted in hospitality? Consider converting your garage or invest in a tiny home to make into an AirBnB! You might also be able to "house hack" by buying a duplex as your primary residence, living in one side and renting out the other side for enough rent to pay your entire mortgage. Real estate is a tremendous hedge against inflation, as you're investing today's dollars in property which, history tells us, is very likely to hold its value as the dollar loses more value each year. As you pay the mortgage each month, based on a purchase price you locked in when the dollar went further, you're investing in your future, using other people's money in the case of rental properties.

   Kathy Fettke, real estate dynamo and author of *Retire Rich with Rentals,* has this word of advice for women like you: "Too often, women have stayed in unhealthy relationships for financial reasons. It does not have to be this way. The more we learn how to earn and invest money, the more freedom we can experience in our lives. Real wealth, the ability to live life on our terms, is worth fighting for." If you're interested in real estate investing, check out Kathy's podcasts in the Resources listed below. You should also check out The Real Estate InvestHer community (www.therealestateinvesther.com), a brain trust of brilliant women sharing real estate investment resources and tips with one another, just how God intended it! Bigger Pockets offers tremendous educational resources and easy-to-understand online investment calculators and other tools at www.biggerpockets.com.

8. **Start a new business**. Were you held back from pursuing business opportunities? Was your creativity squelched during your marriage? Were you discouraged or even ridiculed for your passions? If you are an artist or creative, hone your craft and look into ways to sell what you make! And don't forget to protect your creative works legally. As my friend and personal trademark attorney, Angie Avard Turner, advises creative women all over America, "if it's worth creating, it's worth protecting." There are bad actors out there wanting to knock off your work, so be sure it's protected with all the right contracts, trademarks and other documents.

Are you good with money management or bookkeeping? Offer accounting work from your home or hang a shingle and open a business. There's a great need for honest and thorough bookkeepers and other such professionals providing support services to businesses, as most business owners want to focus on what they do and not the behind-the-scenes busy work that goes along with running the operation.

According to the U.S. Small Business Administration (SBA), there were only 400,000 women-owned businesses in America in 1972. Today, there are over 13 million![2] SBA offers a plethora of resources through its Office of Women's Business Ownership (OWBO) for women entrepreneurs. Moreover, federal funding (grants, low-interest loans) for your new business may also be available to you through SBA. Check it out! There's probably an SBA office near your home.

9. **Work remotely.** There are many ways to earn a solid living in the online space. Are you a seasoned shopper, with an eye for fashion and an Instagram account? Consider becoming an influencer! Some of those ladies are making six figures each year! Good with fashion? Consider an online boutique and start selling clothes on the internet! Know lots of beauty secrets or enjoy sampling new products? I've seen so many people make money just talking to the camera, putting on makeup and posting videos to promote the products they're using. Pinterest can also be a real source of funds if you know how to use it. Staging and photographing home décor products and posting on Pinterest drives increased online sales for big furniture and other décor companies, and these companies will often reward you with a portion of the revenues. I don't know much about it, but there are many articles online about how it works.

Online stores are popping up everywhere, and you can find great success with little expense, from the comfort of your home, with the right marketing. Many people have lucrative stores on

---

[2] https://www.sba.gov/blog/resources-americas-small-businesswomen?utm_medium=email&utm_source=govdelivery

Etsy, Amazon and eBay. The possibilities for women in business in America are endless.

10. **Multiple streams of income are where it's at**. God knows our economy, our weather, our health, and even our very lives are unpredictable. In Ecclesiastes 11:2–6, He cautions us not to put all our eggs in one "income basket": "2Invest in seven ventures, yes, in eight; you do not know what disaster may come upon the land. . . 6sow your seed in the morning, and at evening let not your hands be idle, for you do not know which will succeed, whether this or that, or whether both will do equally well."

I'm a big believer in side hustles and diversifying my investments for this reason. When stocks are down, maybe real estate will remain strong. When one thing makes money, another one may not. But if you're balanced in your approach and always willing to work hard and save/invest what you earn, you'll always be way ahead of the crowd.

As you read this, I'm covering you in prayer that you will be strong and courageous to build a life you love—*your* way. The goal is for your 88-year-old self to look back and be proud of the choices you made at this stage of your life, mindful that, though your heart was hurting and it felt like you were walking with cinder blocks tied to your ankles, you made sound financial decisions which set your course for a stable, successful retirement.

Questions for Reflection

1. Jeremiah 29:11 reminds us: "'For I know the plans I have for you,' declares the Lord, 'plans to prosper you and not to harm you, plans to give you hope and a future.'" Do you believe this for your life today? That (1) there's a plan, (2) it's a plan for you to prosper, (3) it's a plan that will give you hope and a future, and (4) it's a plan that will not harm you? Powerful promises here! Claim them and pray that God will show them to you!

2. Romans 5:3-5 reassures us that ". . . suffering produces endurance, endurance produces character, and character produces hope." How has the Lord started giving you hope in the midst of your suffering? How as your endurance improved as you've struggled? Is your character stronger today than it was before you started your divorce journey? How have you been transformed, for the better?

3. Consider 1 Peter 5:10: "And after you have suffered a little while, the God of all grace, who has called you to his eternal glory in Christ, will himself restore, confirm, strengthen and establish you." Are you starting to see a light at the end of your "suffering tunnel"? Do you feel the Lord restoring you, with a plan to establish you in a new role, with a new purpose for living? Hope for this restoration will keep you going. Do not give up hope!

4. Job had a really rough go for a while, didn't he? He lost all his wealth, his family was destroyed, and he lost his health for a terrible, horrific season. But God's word tells us that "the Lord blessed Job in the second half of his life even more than in the beginning." (Job 42:12, NLT) He'll do the same for you, Dear One, no matter how terrible your suffering has been thus far. A new day is dawning for you!

5. What are your skills? What do you enjoy doing when you have free time? Do you have a degree or special training you can parlay into a career? Who are the mentors around you, both for personal growth and business development tips? Identify your skills, your passions, and your "support people," and you've got a great foundation for your next move! Redeem the time you have on this earth in a big way, Sister!

Resources

Wealth Habits: Six Ordinary Steps to Achieve Extraordinary Financial Freedom—Candy Valentino

Restored: Transforming the Sting of Your Past Into Purpose for Today—Chris Brown

Rich Woman—Kim Kiyosaki

It's Rising Time!—Kim Kiyosaki

The Jennifer Allwood Show—a podcast for creative women in business

Financial Peace—Dave Ramsey

You are a Badass at Making Money—Jen Sincero

The Real Wealth Show with Kathy Fettke

Angie Avard Turner—@angieavardturnerlaw

The Prayer of Jabez—Bruce Wilkinson

www.letsmakeaplan.org (to find a CFP near you)

The Real Estate News for Investors Podcast with Kathy Fettke

Chapter Soundtrack

"Independent Women, Pt. 1" Destiny's Child

"Girl on Fire"—Alicia Keys

"How Do You Like Me Now?"—Toby Keith

"I'm Still Standing"—Elton John

"One Moment in Time"—Whitney Houston

"Is there Life Out There"—Reba McEntire

"She's Gonna Make It"—Garth Brooks

"Survivor"—Destiny's Child

"Her World or Mine"—Michael Ray

"She Works Hard for the Money"—Donna Summer

"Flowers"—Miley Cyrus

"Sit Still, Look Pretty"—Daya

"All I Know So Far"—P!nk

4

Make a New Estate Plan

"A good man leaves an inheritance for his children's children."
— Proverbs 13:22

As a newly single woman, you need to get all your financial affairs in order in the event of your untimely death, especially if you have children. You now have full authority over how your assets and affairs will be managed, and it's important to memorialize your wishes formally so that they'll be carried out in your absence.

Last Will and Testament

A Last Will and Testament, commonly called a "Will," is the legal instrument by which you establish how your assets are divided and how your final arrangements are handled. A Will brings you peace of mind that your wishes will be carried out.

You can also put in your Will your preferences as to guardianship of your children after your death. Should you pass away, there could be a battle of some kind over custody of your children and/or the extent to which your ex must allow your surviving relatives to visit with the children. Your preferences very well may not be binding on the court (they aren't binding where I practice), but it is helpful evidence to be presented of your feelings on the subject should a court ever have to consider custody placements or visitation terms for your kids after you're gone.

Because retirement, brokerage, annuities, and some bank accounts with pay-on-death designees pass as a matter of contract rather than under your will, you need to check with all the managers of these assets to ensure they pass to your chosen beneficiaries upon your death. Too often, people forget to change these beneficiary designations after their divorces, and problems can arise. Consult your attorney with any questions you may have on how to proceed.

Health Care Directives and Financial Agents

You might also consider designating a general agent to manage financial and business matters, and also a health care agent (perhaps the same person) to verbalize your health care decisions in the event you are mentally or physically incapacitated due to illness or injury. Legal instruments to address these circumstances are sometimes called Health Care Directives, Living Wills, Powers of Attorney, or similar names. Ask your lawyer for guidance on whether you need anything like this. And if you already have something in place which gives your ex the power to control your affairs, ask your lawyer how to go about revoking those old documents, stat.

Consider a Trust

There's a good chance your ex could be appointed to manage your estate's assets for the children should you die while they are still minors. If you predict you'll be turning over in your grave if this happens, you should consider leaving your assets to a trust for the children's benefit, with a trustee you trust being assigned to manage the money to ensure the children's best interests are served. Talk to a competent estate planning attorney in your area to consider your options.

Plan for College

Don't assume your ex and/or his family will keep their word to your children after your divorce. For example, say your husband's family set up a trust for the college education costs of all their grandchildren, and, in reliance on this promise, you've never saved for the children's college expenses. If your ex and his family do not commit in the final divorce agreement for this trust to remain applicable to your children, you need to start saving for college right away, just in case they renege. I've seen it happen, friend, and talk about a shock! It's amazing how grandparents' attitudes can change after a divorce, and they could try to punish *you* by making you fund the college costs without any help from them. Your decision to walk away from Golden Boy could bring out the worst in your ex and his family. Hope for the best that they will keep their word to your little ones, but you must be ready—with a plan of your own—in case they don't.

With the assistance of a good estate planning attorney and your financial planner, you can establish an estate plan to cover all contingencies. Rely on their wisdom!

Questions for Reflection

1. Did you have a Will when you were married to Mr. Used-to-be-Wonderful? How does that Will need to change now that you're single? Are your priorities different than before? What would you include in your new Will to establish your particular preferences?
2. Do you have a health care agent? Do you have particular preferences about end-of-life care or who you'd like to have speaking with doctors on your behalf?
3. Do you have a solid, trustworthy plan for your children's education costs after high school?

Resources

Savvy Estate Planning—James L. Cunningham, Jr.

The You Plan—Michelle Borquez | Connie Wetzell

Estate Planning Success Just for Women—Lynne Marie Kohm

Chapter Soundtrack

"Dreams"—Fleetwood Mac

"Legacy"—Nichole Nordeman

5

Dads are Important

I was just eight years old when my parents separated. My mom and I moved to a town over two hours away for her to start an exciting new business while my dad remained in our hometown to start over without us. My dad, who I called "Diddy" in my little-girl-Southern accent, was struggling at the time. Within the nine-month period surrounding my parents' separation, his mother died, his home burned to the ground with all his belongings inside, and he went bankrupt farming pecans. His 12-year marriage was over, and his only child wasn't there anymore.

He was working as a coach and teacher at the local high school while going back to college to advance his career as an educator, barely scraping by while my parents' divorce was pending. He later told me his only meal each day during that time was lunch at the school cafeteria, as he was trying to save every penny.

My dad promised he would spend as much time as he could with me, despite the distance. He really couldn't afford the gas, but he found a way to pick me up and bring me back, doing all the driving both ways, almost every weekend. My mom was generous in sharing time with him, and he took every minute of parenting time he could get. He never stopped showing up.

Those car trips with him formed some of my most precious memories. We spent hours talking in the car about the important things, listening to *America's Top 40 Countdown* on Sundays, and (on a special day every now and then) stopping to eat at the Shoney's off the I-75 exit.

He had a florist deliver a stuffed frog with hearts for eyes, tied with balloons, to my third-grade classroom on Valentine's Day that first year I was away from him. The card read, "Happy Valentine's, baby! Daddy loves you." I still have the card. And the frog.

As I got older, he taught me to hunt deer, let me be his retriever at dove shoots and taught me how to shoot a basketball. He made me the most amazing, towering Dagwood sandwiches out of white bread, bacon and all the fixings. We ate Breyer's peach ice cream together from the carton. He taught me to build a fire and a vegetable garden. He let me drive his old truck to the trash dump before I had a license, "just to practice."

We played gin rummy on the living room floor, and I would laugh hysterically as he strutted around the room with one finger in the air after beating me, which he often did. But he always allowed a rematch when I demanded one. And he'd let me win that one every time.

He taught me to bait a hook and cast a line with a Zebco 33 from Wal-Mart. He taught me to love Larry Munson, Vince Dooley and the Georgia Bulldogs.

He got me a used set of golf clubs and taught me to play at the local course, where he never said no when I wanted a cold can of Gatorade from the machine after the first nine holes. He made me redo homework assignments until they were right. I rode with him on a scooter through the hot cotton fields of South Georgia while he looked for insects and reported back to farmers. I've never seen anyone work so hard. Before I went to college, he showed me how to check the oil. And when I sprung my post-graduation summer wedding plans on him, he didn't object. He just took an additional job to pay for it, and never complained one time.

Dads are Important | 33

I saw how he took care of my stepmother when her health was failing, and we grieved together after she drew her last breath. He was by my side every day as I walked through the pain of my divorce. A girl needs her dad even more in the hard times.

He never was one to throw around Bible verses or "get preachy" in parenting. Instead, he *showed* me fruits of the spirit by the way he lived his life of goodness, patience, kindness, gentleness, and self-control.

He told me I could do anything I set my mind to do, that I was smart and capable. That I was so very loved. Every little girl or boy needs that kind of foundation, one that makes them know in their bones that they have what it takes to succeed, to know that someone has their back and believes in them. I have never doubted any of it for even one second.

I always tell my lady clients to count themselves blessed if they have a guy like my dad for a coparent. Kids need to feel the love of *both* parents during and after a divorce more than they did before.

You may be the best mom in the world, but you will never be your child's dad.

The experts say boys get their sense of how to be man from their fathers, and that girls get their self-esteem from the way their fathers love them. Dads have a special parenting role you can't fill.

My parents certainly had their differences when I was young, but they coparented beautifully and, still today, remain good friends. When they attend holiday celebrations at my home each year, there are always lots of laughs . . . not a single sign of a grudge or any bitterness. That should be the goal of everyone who divorces, to put differences aside and set an example of kindness and relational reconciliation for the next generations to witness. Beauty from ashes.

Divorced ladies, why do you so often want your ex to fail at parenting? I see it all the time in my line of work. Root for him, not against him. Your child's father may have deeply hurt you. Maybe he was a horrible husband and did things you can't quite get over. I get it. But when you're tempted, out of your own sadness, to withhold your child from him, think again. Your child needs a daddy, even if he isn't perfect, so long as the relationship can be safe for the child. I've seen it many times in my practice . . . some of the worst husbands are the best fathers! Pray that God will make him an excellent example and a wise, attentive parent.

Rather than hoping your ex fails so others will regard you as the "better parent," (whatever that is), do what you can to set him up for success! Give him extra parenting time when he asks for it if the kids want to go. Tell him about the upcoming school programs so he can plan to be there. Send him copies of the report cards. Invite him to parent-teacher conferences if you both can be cordial. Buy him a Father's Day gift from the children each year, if he'll accept it from you. Make sure the kids support him in the things he pursues. Don't show your fanny if they sit with him at events you're both attending, even if it's "your day"; it's not all about you.

While this type of coparenting is the ideal, there are some toxic situations in which coparenting is <u>impossible</u> due to a history of abusive behavior. When this is the case, you should try parallel parenting—parenting in two homes with minimum interactions and contact between parents, just to keep tensions down for everyone involved. It's necessary to have appropriate boundaries when interactions with a coparent are harmful to you or the children. I was blessed to grow up with a positive dynamic, but not all folks are.

When you speak of him to your children, focus on his good qualities, and vent frustrations to your friends or your mama instead of burdening your kids with them. Acknowledge his new love interest and let her know you appreciate her kindness to your children. Make them attend his second wedding looking presentable. Rise above your own feelings and try to give him the benefit of the doubt whenever possible. Model this kind of class and character for your children.

Those babies need to believe their dad is amazing (even if he hasn't been so great to you), for they are half him, and they need to feel like they come from good stock. Give your children the freedom to love and revere their dad. They only get one.

Questions for Reflection

1. What kind of relationship do you have with your own father? How does that relationship impact how you encourage your children's relationship with their father? Are you holding onto any unhealthy baggage from your childhood as you endeavor to coparent with your ex?
2. Did your ex deeply hurt you? Leviticus 19:18 tells us not to "take vengeance, nor bear any grudge . . . but you shall love your neighbor as yourself; I am the Lord." Hebrews 12:15 tells us, "See to it that no one comes short of the grace of God; that no root of bitterness springing up causes trouble, and by it many be defiled." When you're tempted to use the children as a weapon to get back at your ex, how can remembering these verses help you rise above hurt feelings in promoting a great relationship between your kids and their dad?
3. What are some things you can do to help your children know it's okay to love their dad? Have you made it clear that it's not a competition, that they are free to love you both? Do you remind them every day how much both parents love them?
4. How is communication going with your ex? How can you raise the level of discourse, for your children's sake? How can you make him know you value his position in the kids' lives?

5. Has your ex harassed or abused you? If so, what appropriate boundaries can you erect to shield yourself from further abuse, while also allowing him to parent the children? Would going to email-only contact, the use of coparenting phone applications, or a lawyer's help ease the current tensions without negatively impacting the children's relationship with him?

Chapter Soundtrack

"Highway 20 Ride"—Zac Brown Band
"Butterfly Kisses"—Bob Carlisle
"Drive (for Daddy Gene)"—Alan Jackson
"I'm Already There"—Lonestar
"I Don't Call Him Daddy"—Doug Supernaw

6

Coparenting and Counterparenting: Architecture, Not Archeology

"Let us not become weary in doing good, for at the proper time we will reap a harvest if we do not give up."
—Galatians 6:9

Divorce is often unavoidable. If you aren't able to give your kids an intact nuclear family, you should do everything within your power to bless them with happy memories and a solid foundation in two homes. It takes cooperation, humility, kindness, selflessness and a lot of grace to get it right.

Good Coparents are Architects

Skyscraper erectors don't focus on what's underground after the foundation is laid. They're focused on building upward, on making progress above ground. They're considering the work still to be done to complete the project, rather than the tasks already behind them. The same approach applies to coparenting with your ex. Despite your past differences, you still share the common task of raising your children. It's the most important task of your life.

Building your children up to be independent adults of outstanding character is the task at hand, the common labor of coparenting. The old saying about it taking a village to raise children rings true, and you realize that more and more as your children age and their needs increase. Children need all the love and support around them they can get.

You and your ex are now out of the marriage business, but you're still in business constructing little humans together. When children are still young, a good parent, like a good architect, draws a mental plan for the kind of child they want to raise, and then gets to work guiding that child on a path toward a moral, well-adjusted adulthood. You must do everything in your power to foster a positive coparenting relationship with your ex. The children didn't ask for your divorce, and you have a duty to your children to make their experience in two homes the best it can be.

One thing is certain: you will never have a quality relationship with your coparent if you live in the past. You can't focus on all the ways your ex wounded you. You must find it in yourself to lick your wounds one last time, compartmentalize them somehow in your brain, and focus only on the coparenting part of your relationship with him, resolutely and selflessly focused on your children's well-being. Your kids need you to move on and get over it already.

Lose the Archeology Mindset

If you're still hurting from your divorce, it can be hard to forgive and move on. Unforgiveness brings grudges, and grudges make you bitter, hindering your future relationships and preventing you from fulfilling God's purpose in your life. Much like an archeologist digging up and analyzing dead things, a parent who cannot let go of the past constantly brings up the negative memories of the breakup, how badly they perceive the other parent to have treated them before the divorce, and the character flaws of the other parent. Parents in this sort of dynamic naturally and regularly encounter serious communication breakdown. After all, how can you have rational conversation with a person about a child's needs when all they want to talk about is their personal vendetta against you as a human being?

This kind of mindset can ruin your children's childhood. Here are the destructive behaviors you'll get from this kind of coparent:

1. **They cannot be courteous** (let alone kind or considerate) toward you, not even on the most joyous occasions for the children. The hatred and resentment for you runs so deep that *your very presence* makes them lose all control over their emotions.

2. **They take everything you do as a personal attack**, refusing to give you any grace or benefit of the doubt, to a ridiculous degree. The coparent doing archeology is easily offended.

3. **They make everything a competition with their coparent**, viewing coparenting as a zero-sum game where one parent must lose and the other must win. They inhabit a world of absolutes with no room for common ground, understanding, or any effort to compromise for the sake of harmony.

4. **Always the Victim.** The archaeologist coparent is always the victim of their own story, and the other parent is—you guessed it—always the villain. They want nothing more than to create a negative public view of you, making you out to be the "bad one." More often than not, this victim roleplaying morphs into the combative parent seeking emotional support from the kids and doing their level best to alienate the children from the other parent. In the mind of the archaeologist coparent, parenting is a competition with distinctly opposite "sides," and the children are expected to choose whose side they're on. The winner gets the kids' loyalty.

5. **They refuse to pay what they owe.** Archaeologist coparents often refuse to pull their financial weight for the children. If your ex withdraws from parenting like this, it's usually payback for some perceived wrong he genuinely believes you've inflicted on

him, and thus you deserve the financial hardship he's creating for you. The saddest part of this kind of treatment is that the children ultimately suffer from the lack of resources. All your son wants is to know is that he'll have what he needs for baseball next week. And your daughter just needs to know she'll have a Homecoming dress and cute shoes so she can fit in at the dance. The level-headed, empathetic coparent is usually the one who ends up unfairly sacrificing to get what the children need so that their angst is assuaged.

Respectful Communication and Appropriate Boundaries are Key

The archaeologist coparent refuses to communicate productively or respectfully, always picking a fight or turning the conversation to past interactions which have no relevance to the matter currently being discussed. All a child wants is to feel like his parents have it together and are a somewhat united front, and for this to occur, you must be capable of mature communication free of personal attacks and threatening language. It's not about you and your ex anymore. All of your energy must be directed at bringing up your children to be loving, others-focused, mentally stable adults. If you are incapable of having cordial conversation with one another about parenting matters, or if you cannot listen to the other parent's opinions on parenting matters with an open, respectful mind, let me tell you, your children deserve better.

It's also important to understand that your ex isn't going to parent the children the same way you do. You have got to release control over how he parents if you're going to proceed in peace. You must accept that you have no control over what happens at his house and give him a chance to figure it out without your meddling. He may not be a perfect parent, but neither are you! Let him be their dad, in his own way. Do not interfere unless the children are in danger, and **always defer to your lawyer** on how best to proceed in such a case.

You only get a certain number of tickets to the high school graduation ceremony, and you will have to see your coparent many times before you die. There will be awards ceremonies, parent-teacher conferences, Senior Night in sports, college graduation, your children's weddings, the births of your grandchildren, and the list goes on.

Your goal should be to have a good enough relationship with your former spouse that you can sit in the same row at graduations and weddings, celebrating each milestone together, sharing in the pride of the lovely adult you constructed as a team after you finally put your personal differences aside. Your kids will thank you for it.

Coparenting with a Crazy Person

After you've separated and relieved yourself of the stress of living with your ex, having to share your children with him may be the hardest thing you'll ever do. A quarrelsome coparent often has trouble controlling his emotions and withholds coparenting cooperation solely as a way of intentionally frustrating or punishing you. When such a dynamic emerges, you have to fight for the child's well-being as your ex fights for *control*.

It's a terrible shame to wish away your children's childhood just so you won't have to deal with a combative coparent any longer. Coparenting does not have to be difficult, and it isn't hard for well-adjusted adults. Diagnosed narcissists and others with abusive tendencies, however, are simply incapable of seeing past their own perceived victim status to consider the child's best interest when dealing with the other parent. They hate the other parent more than they love their children. If you're one of the unlucky few who drew an unstable coparent in the Game of Life, you have a long road ahead.

Pollyanna's Story

When Patrick and I divorced, I just knew we could be the best coparents to our kids, Paul and Pearl. Patrick had been unfaithful years earlier, and we'd just never gotten over it. He kept doing things to make me not trust him, and, in his resentment toward me for being unable to "just get over it already," he would lash out in anger. It was unhealthy for the children, and I couldn't take it anymore, but we'd never disagreed even once about decisions for the children. I knew we'd be happier apart and had every confidence the children would also be happier in two homes than in the one we shared. I believed that separation would take the tension away and equip us to have more rational discussions.

So, it came as a shock when, as soon as we separated, Patrick kept something stirred up with me all the time. He made everything a battle! He took everything I said in coparenting as a personal attack against him, and then he'd yell at me and call me names. It could be something as simple as my texting him Paul's soccer schedule for the week or the dosage of Pearl's ear infection prescription. He took immediate offense, accusing me of talking to him like a child, saying "don't you think I know how to give Pearl her medicine? I've got my s*#t together. Stop texting me this nonsense." Then other times, out of the blue, he would send me sweet texts or call me saying in a loving tone how he thought we'd made a terrible mistake, and we should get back together immediately. When I would deflect the question or change the subject, he would start cursing me at the top of his lungs, calling me ugly names and hang up on me. These calls and texts would come in late at night after he'd been drinking, and they would be so relentless that I'd have to silence my cell phone in order to get any rest.

He would pressure the children to try to convince me to take him back. After we'd divided all our marital property in the divorce, he'd have the kids secretly steal things like blankets and snorkel gear from my cabinets and closets for him to keep at his house. He'd withhold information I needed about school or the kids' activities if he happened to receive it first, and then he'd revel in victory when I would miss some important thing and look like the worst mom ever. He would threaten not to return the children to me as the court order required, and I'd have to pay my lawyer to call or write him letters.

He'd tell the kids they didn't have to follow my rules, and he'd ask them to lie about eating M&Ms for dinner and having no set bedtime at his house. He would keep the nice clothes I bought the kids at his house and refuse to return them, opting instead to return the children in stained or too-small clothing. He wanted me to have to buy new clothes for the kids constantly, I suppose as a punishment for leaving him. He'd text or call demanding that the kids communicate with him, at times he knew full well *they were at practice or at a friend's house, and sometimes even* when I was at work and the kids were at school, *just to create a record to support his allegation that I wouldn't let him talk to his kids.* He would also demand information about the children that he already had *from the school or the coach, just to create a narrative that I refused to cooperate with him.*

My therapist taught me how to respond calmly and keep control of my communications with Patrick. On her advice, I would cordially respond to his incessant text messages with something like, "Thank you for your patience; I was at work when you texted. Please see my texts and emails earlier this week on the requested topics. The kids are doing great today; their grades are available in the school's online parent portal. I sent you the login instructions on August 2, but I'm happy to send it again if you can't locate it. I'll have the kids call you this evening. They'll be so excited to tell you about their day." And the more composed I remained, the madder he got.

He became a master of manipulating situations to make him look like the victim. He'd ask to get the kids later than the time set in the court papers, and when I would agree, he would claim he never asked to move the time and accuse me of withholding the children from him. After that, there was no way I could trust him to adjust the schedule by agreement, so I had to stick by the papers. Another example was when he'd go radio silent for a few weeks, never calling even to check on the children, and then accuse me of alienating them from him or prohibiting contact with the kids.

He started stalking my location using the children's iPads, and he'd use Facetime calls as an opportunity to see inside my home environment and to see who else was spending time there. I'd get screenshots from his Facetime calls with the kids where he'd photographed my pile of freshly-washed-but-yet-unfolded laundry on the couch as evidence of my poor homemaking skills and unfitness to parent.

Patrick's counterparenting attacks became 1000 percent worse when I started dating again. He heard I'd gone on a date and told the children about my new friend before I wanted them to know, trying to convince the children that I shouldn't be dating. He'd told the kids "Mama's an adulteress," and that I was replacing them with a man. He also told the children my new friend was a child molester and began citing stats to Pearl about how common it is for stepfathers to sexually molest their stepdaughters. Pearl was then naturally apprehensive about meeting my friend, let alone having him get to know her at all. He would tell Paul not to get too close to my friend, for Patrick was his only "real dad," that this new guy wanted to take Patrick's place, and that Paul owed Patrick a duty of loyalty no to let my friend get too close. The kids never left my primary care, but Patrick kept the pressure on for them to come and live with him. It cost me over $5,000.00 in legal fees to fight off Patrick's custody challenge.

While Patrick took great issue with my dating someone steady, he had a revolving door of different women staying at his house. The children would get attached to someone new, and then he'd break up with each one.

I tried every approach imaginable to coparenting with Patrick. When I was cordial, he accused me of being "fake-nice" and would tell me to shut up and not insult his intelligence. When I stood up for myself, called out his behavior as irrational and unacceptable and tried to erect appropriate communication and other interpersonal boundaries, he'd go crazy on me all the more, demanding that I communicate with him and accusing me of refusing to coparent. When I would lose composure and yell back at him to leave me alone or call him a name, we would get into shouting matches, and he would say I was a gaslighter and a narcissist, and that he *was the victim in our relationship. I couldn't win. The children were suffering. And I was so demoralized over my inability to crack the code to positive coparenting. What was I doing wrong? What could I be doing differently? I'm a smart woman and a friendly person. Why was I failing at coparenting?*

My therapist and attorney taught me about parallel parenting, and I found that worked better than any other approach I'd tried to that point. Minimizing contact kept tensions down for the kids and also for me.

I blocked Patrick's number on the advice of law enforcement officials after the harassment escalated, and imposing an email-only communication policy seemed to deter most of the meanness I had previously received over knee-jerk text messages. I suppose emails require a little more time to compose, and his brain would kick into gear and control his emotions better than with texts. I responded to each email he sent, but I could tell Patrick didn't like losing the ability to harass me that phone and text messages had given him.

Things came to a head one Thursday night when Patrick came to my house after the kids were in bed, banging on my front door and shouting my name, demanding I come out and talk to him. I was on the phone with the 911 dispatcher when policemen arrived and arrested him for disorderly conduct and criminal trespass. The arrest was a rude awakening, but that's what was necessary to get his attention and make him leave me alone.

If Your Ex is a Quarrelsome Coparent

It's hard to know how to deal with a coparent who wants you to fail and hates you more than he loves the children. Here are some things you can do to protect yourself from the schemes of a difficult coparent:

1. **Keep a detailed coparenting journal.** Write down every significant detail from each day of your coparenting journey so that you can coherently articulate all events if you end up in court. If he disparaged you, withheld communication, did something that made the children feel unsafe, yelled at you, neglected the children's needs, or anything else you may need to tell a judge one day, make an accurate record of it, and prepare to support your coparenting journal with recordings, documents, messages and any other legal proof you have of the events.

2. **Exclude him from your space and control communications.** If your ex creates constant controversy, consider erecting some boundaries to preserve your peace. If he comes into your house without an invitation when he picks up the children, raises his voice or otherwise intimidates you on your property, make him stay at the mailbox or meet you at the police station for exchanges. If he acts ugly in public, make it a policy not to go near his space. If he's hateful to you on the phone or on text, insist that he communicate with you only through a coparenting app like Our Family Wizard which diffuses tensions and quells abusive language between parents.

3. **Don't negotiate with a terrorist.** During the Iran hostage crisis, Ronald Reagan famously said, "We don't negotiate with terrorists." American foreign policy was built around this principle, and its wisdom likewise applies to coparenting with a crazy man. You, a rational human, believe you can reason with anyone and

they'll see things your way if only you explain it well enough. Dear One, do not deceive yourself and waste valuable time once it's clear you're dealing with a coparent incapable of level-headed reason. Each word you throw his way gives him your energy, and your energy—even if it's not all positive—is what he feeds on! All he wants is to pull you into some long battle so that he can keep your attention. Your energy only feeds the beast and promotes further nonsense, as he lives to get a rise out of you. Once he's shown you he's incapable of fairness or compromise, you have to step away from his games altogether, limit communication and guard your heart.

4. **Keep it cordial and professional.** Do not communicate with your ex when you're triggered or upset, and never after you've been drinking. Only reply to things that require a response and get comfortable with silence. If you need to reply to a substantive message from him, do it only in writing, and, unless it's an emergency in need of immediate reply, let things sit a while before you respond to allow time for emotions to simmer down. If you're discussing the children and he tries to take the conversation to a personal or romantic place, shut it down. He needs to recognize he no longer has that kind of access to you.

5. **Employ a strict, written-communication-only policy.** If it gets bad enough, you may need to cut out all verbal or phone communication with your ex to prevent him from twisting your words and go to an all-in-writing or email-only communication policy. It's just a business relationship now; you're in the business of raising children, and this is your only connection with him. It's so much easier to fire off an offensive text message than it is to send a mean email, and each text can have you

jumping with PTSD and anxiety. With email, the time it takes a person to enter the email address, subject line and body of the message serves as a cooling-off period not present with text messaging. If he sends harassing texts, consider creating a new email address dedicated only to coparenting conversations so that your regular email isn't clogged with messages from him. Emails are easier than texts are to print and make great evidence, should you ever need them in court.

Try Parallel Parenting

Coparenting only works if parents can stay on reasonably good terms. In high-conflict parenting scenarios, one way to keep stress down for the children is to employ a parallel parenting approach in which the parents consult one another only on the major decisions and otherwise interact as little as possible. In parallel parenting, each parent raises the child as he/she wishes in each individual home, custody swaps are done at school or sports practice (with one party dropping the child off and the other party picking up the child at the end of the school day or event), there's a strict calendar both sides follow, and there are guidelines about how decisions will be made, and disagreements resolved. All of these measures minimize conflict and promote healthy, painless conflict resolution when conflicts do arise.

Supporting Children through High-Conflict Coparenting

So how can you help your children cope with high-conflict coparenting?

1. **Give them the freedom to love their dad.** If he's a good dad, your kids are better for it, even if he's the worst coparent the world ever saw. Rather than being jealous, enthusiastically listen as the kids tell you about their vacations with him, as they show you the

gifts he gives them, as he introduces them to new hobbies and life-enriching activities. Be thankful for each blessing the children receive! Don't undermine him or make it a competition by requiring the children to call your house "home" and Dad's house "Dad's house." It's okay for them to have two places to call home. Two Christmases should be celebrated as the biggest perk of two homes, not a reason for them to see you sad and weepy over sharing parenting time. Give them grace to find joy in their new normal wherever it shows up. They're adjusting just like you are!

2. **Be their safe place to land.** If your ex is hyperemotional or codependent on the children for support or validation, or if he disparages you to the children during visits with him, your children may come back to you with all kinds of emotions and energy to sort out. If they lash out at you during this process, let them. Let them get it all out and consider it a compliment instead of being offended. Don't you see? They feel *safe* with you, safe enough to be raw and real and to tell you how they really feel, even when it isn't pretty. You're the only safe place they have to be honest and vent their feelings, for Dad would never tolerate it. Allow yourself to be the whipping post in these brief times. Experts say they usually pass quickly.

When children express fear about being at Dad's or any discomfort about visitation time, they may want to establish code words or emojis they can text you if they're ever feeling unsafe at Dad's and need you to intervene. For example, one client told her son to text her an emoji of an apple if ever he felt unsafe with his father. When the child sent an emoji of a house, that meant the child was home alone with no supervision and was afraid. The upside-down smiley face emoji meant that Dad wasn't letting the child call his mother. The emoji of fireworks meant Dad and his girlfriend are fighting. An example of a code word/safety statement could be something innocuous like, "Mom, can we bake cookies when I get back from Dad's?" Such a statement wouldn't raise alarm should your ex see or hear it but will let you know if your child is in distress.

3. **Support the kids without disparaging Dad.** You can support the children without badmouthing their dad. Coparenting is not a competition, and there's no good to come from involving children in your coparenting arguments. If they are privy to your parental discord, they will be anxious, worry about you and/or your ex, and be unable to function normally under the stress of it all. Kids don't need to know if his child support payment is late or he's making poor choices. Insulate them! They need to feel like the adults in their lives have it covered.

4. **Present a united front.** Don't allow the kids to play you against one another.

    Do not allow them to speak of him disrespectfully. Kids are little geniuses and detect chinks in the parental armor almost immediately. If they sense you and Dad aren't a team, they are sure to try to play you against one another. If possible, stay united with uniform rules for the children's best interests. And unless your ex is abusing the children or exposing them to danger, do not allow your child to leave his house during his allotted parenting time. You wouldn't want him encouraging the children to leave your house early, so don't do that to him.

5. **Prepare for parental alienation (and to be accused of it).** If your ex is alienating the child from you by disparaging your character or allowing others to do so in the child's presence,

you have to refute the negative comments with your *actions*, to *show* the child that you are not the person you've been depicted to be, and without saying anything negative about the other parent. It's a very tricky balance and difficult to maneuver, and it can sometimes be many years before you see the tide turn. But children ultimately see the truth of things if you can just stay the course, no matter how difficult that is, and when they do, they naturally don't want to spend as much time with the alienator. Moreover, if your ex tries to turn your kids against you, the children may eventually resent him for it and distance themselves from his abuse, and *you will be blamed.* This is why it's so important always to be kind and cordial with your ex. Even in your weakest moments when he's pushed all your buttons, but you mustn't give him any factual basis for showing that you might be an alienator.

Some parents are so nonconfrontational that they'll categorically disengage from all possible contact with a combative coparent, even if it means never coming to the child's public activities. You need to keep showing up for your children's events. Do not let your insecurities keep you home; your children need you there to support them, no matter how uncomfortable it may be for you.

With a little courage and a lot of prayer, you'll get through your children's childhood, no matter how awful your ex may be. Trust the Lord with your coparenting path, and He will make it straight.

Questions for Reflection

1. A 2021 *Journal of Family Medicine* study found that abusers use the children to:

    stay in their coparents' lives (76%), intimidate them (72%), keep track of them (72%), harass them (71%), or frighten them (69%). Others surveyed said their abusive coparent tried to turn the children against them (62%) or used the children to try to take them back and resume the romantic relationship (45%). Have you suffered any of these since your separation? How have you dealt with it? What has worked, and what hasn't worked? What kinds of measures can you consider implementing from this book to address these issues?

2. God tells us in Isaiah 49:25 that He "will fight the one who fights you and I will save your children." Do you believe Him? Do you know in your bones that God loves your little ones even more than you do?

3. How has your ex used the children to harass, punish or intimidate you? How did you respond? How can you respond differently for a better, more peaceful outcome?

4. Does your ex seem to gain energy the more you respond to his attacks? How can you respond differently next time, with compassion and kindness, to keep him from baiting you into behavior you'll regret?

5. Does your ex have a way of manipulating situations to make him appear to be a victim? What can you do to keep this from happening? How can you use the parallel parenting concept to ease the tensions of coparenting?

Resources

The Parallel Parenting Solution—Carl Knickerbocker, J.D.

Parallel Parenting—The Only Way to Coparent with a Narcissist: Managing a Counter Parent, Setting Boundaries, and Protecting Your Child from Parental Alienation—Wendy Carter

SPLIT (the movie)—www.splitfilm.org

Set Boundaries, Find Peace—Nedra Glover Tawwab

Love and Logic: Online Parenting Course—www.loveandlogic.com

The Narcissist Trauma Recovery Podcast with Caroline Strawson— Episodes 076 and 034

Danish Bashir—@narcabusecoach on Instagram

Chapter Soundtrack

"Next Thing You Know"—Jordan Davis

7

Get Your Groove Back: Modern Dating

"It was when I was happiest that I longed most... The sweetest thing in all my life has been the longing... to find the place where all the beauty came from."
—C.S. Lewis, *Till We Have Faces*

The Lost Years Will be Restored to You

Joel 2:25 promises God will "restore to you the years the swarming locusts have eaten." Dear Friend, do not doubt He is at work, restoring the years you lost, holding in store for you an extraordinary new life you will love.

The divorce process is a heavy weight on your shoulders, and it's sometimes easy to lose hope that your life will ever be happy again. I had this fear during my divorce, and many of my clients have had it, too.

How quickly we forget that God is in the business of transforming lives! He has a plan for each of us, even when we can't see it. Even when it hurts. Even when we are at our most hopeless. You are never too old to find happiness. As long as you're alive, the possibility of a better day is always possible. This uncoupling is not the end of your life.

You Don't *Need* a Man to be Happy

There's no rule that says you have to be married or in a romantic relationship to be happy. You may even find that you enjoy the solitude for a while, maybe for the rest of your life!

For over 85 years, Harvard has been studying what makes people happy and helps us live longer. You know what they've found makes people consistently happier and keeps us healthier than anything else? Meaningful social connections and close personal relationships, but not necessarily marriage. The study found that while relationships are the primary key to happiness, *marital status* doesn't dictate happiness. Harvard also discovered the *quality* of our relationships is more important than the *number* of relationships we have.[3]

No woman *requires* a man in order to have a fulfilling life. She just needs to surround herself with warm, supportive relationships. But while this is certainly true, some women are just hardwired to prefer the married life over the single life. They like having a life partner, someone to bless the household with their gifts and contribution, someone with whom to share life's ups and downs, someone to bless and encourage. There's nothing wrong with that.

I was happier than I've ever been during my time of singleness after my separation from Mark, but the happiness, peace and hopeful expectation of that season was fully eclipsed by the lasting joy I found once I met my second husband. Before I met him, I honestly believed every married person I knew was just pretending to be happy and silently struggling like me. I cynically deemed the idea of marriage truly ever being happy was nothing more than a farce. It's amazing how you can think you have things all figured out, but then God shows up and shows you a whole new life.

---

[3] Robert Waldinger, Marc Schulz. *The Good Life: Lessons from the World's Longest Scientific Study of Happiness* (2023).

Heal and Don't Look Back

You'll never find the abundant life God has for you—whether coupled up or single—until you've sorted out the emotions of the past and left them there.

I had an illustrated children's Bible when I was little, and in it was a full-color image of Lot's wife after God turned her into a pillar of salt, along with the story of how it happened because she simply looked back at the city of Sodom as she and her family were fleeing its destruction. God had told her *not to look back*, something I thought at the time to be a perfectly normal thing to want to do if you're leaving home. As a child, I just didn't quite understand how a loving God would just turn a woman into salt over one glance over her shoulder. It didn't seem fair.

But when you delve into the original Genesis 19 text a little more deeply, you find that the word for "looking" used there is *tābeṭ*, which means something different than other Hebrew words for "looking." The Hebrew "*tābeṭ*" means to look back *with longing*. It's apparent Lot's wife didn't just look back at the evil city of Sodom all willy-nilly, but rather with a desire in her heart to *go back* there. God had benevolently instructed the family to flee for their lives, not to look behind them, to move quickly and not to stop, lest they be swept away—not too much to ask to preserve your life and limb, if you ask me—and here's Lot's wife looking back anyway, thus revealing the true condition of her heart. Lot's wife *loved* that city and didn't *want* to leave it, even after God had told her it wasn't good for her to stay there.

When Jesus tells us in Luke 17:32 to "remember Lot's wife," he's telling us not to long for things that are unhealthy for us or contrary to God's best plans for our lives.

Have you ever just *had to have* something (or someone) you *knew* wasn't good for you? Like Lot's wife, too many of us look back at toxic marriages *with longing*. So often, we look back and yearn for the unhealthy things in our rearview mirrors and, in doing so, are immobilized just like Lot's wife, unable to move forward. So many women rob themselves of today's joy and tomorrow's promise by clinging to the past.

It's natural to remember the good times, and it's healthy to be thankful for those positive things (like children) that came from your marriage, but don't ever let yourself look back at your broken marriage with longing. There's a reason that chapter is closed. God tells us that He's *doing a new thing*, causing streams to spring up in the desert to bless us.[4] Release that longing to the Lord, and—believe you me—he will replace it with something else. Turn that page! There's something better just around the corner.

If you want to date, there are billions of men in the world, and you can date. You will not be alone unless you just want to be! Like my dear stepmother always said, "Men are like MARTA busses. Another one is coming around every five minutes." The trick, I believe, is getting yourself into the right mindset to welcome new love with openness and authenticity, so that you connect in a healthy way with a new life partner. Getting your heart and mind healthy and whole again after divorce is much harder than finding a person to go out with. Years of dealing with people in your position (and being one myself) have taught me this time of healing is the most sacred part of the journey. It's you and God, a sacred working out of all your past hurts until, over time, you're renewed and whole again, with the confidence you need to go on, with hopeful expectation as you consider the next chapter. This period of my life with Jesus was ever so precious, for it was then that I drew nearest the Throne and felt Him like a salve on my deepest wounds. Once you've known Jesus like that, you will never doubt His presence ever again.

---

4   *See* Isaiah 43:19 and Isaiah 35:67.

You Are Not Too Old, and It Is Not Too Late

You are not too old, and it is never too late for:

- ❖ *New adventures*
- ❖ *New friendships*
- ❖ *New romance*
- ❖ *New ways to serve and connect with others*
- ❖ *Fresh starts*

Age is truly just a number. Many fear dating after divorce, saying "all the good ones are taken" or, "I'm too old for anyone to want me." What nonsense! You are not unlovable just because one person didn't know how to love you. I've had clients in their seventies and even eighties find soulmates after divorce. Don't ever think it can't happen to you.

God could be waiting to bless you with new love at any moment. He may have the most perfect mate waiting for you when your heart is ready. You just have to heal from this wound first. Psalm 147:3 tells us the Lord heals the brokenhearted and binds up their wounds.

It's a big world. There are plenty of people out there looking for love and connection; I know because I meet them every day. Heal from your heartbreak, grow in your faith, serve your family and your fellow man. Be open to good things. Love others big and watch that love come right back to you.

Isaiah 31:3 speaks of God's blessing and promise to those who grieve—to give them "beauty instead of ashes, the oil of joy instead of mourning, and a garment of praise instead of a spirit of despair" and to make us "oaks of righteousness, a planting of the Lord for the display of his splendor." It's easy to think you've wasted part of your life on the marriage that's now ending. But every bit of the chapter that's closing got you to the place you are today.

Guard Your Heart and Mind Your Soul Ties

If you've been starved for affection in your marriage, the first bit of kindness from a guy is going to feel really good, and you may find yourself falling into an intoxicating romance. As you begin to enjoy your life again and meeting interesting new men, remember to protect your good name and your tender heart.

Casual sex just isn't God's best for us, Friend. Science tells us physical intimacy brings about powerful oxytocin neurohormone releases which bring on the euphoria of feeling like you're "in love" and bond you tightly to the one you're with. Some people call this bond a "soul tie," and although I can't find evidence of that particular concept in the scriptures, it makes sense that sex would naturally create a permanent connection between parties, based only on the sheer strength of the brain chemicals released with the act. When two people have sex, the Bible tells us they become "one flesh." If those two who are so tightly bonded don't end up staying together, the heartbreak can be soul-shattering. Anyone who's suffered a bad breakup knows what I'm talking about; the rejection can destroy your confidence. Be careful with your soul ties and manage temptation so that your good reputation stays good, and nothing hinders your intimate relationship with God.

What Kind of Guy Should I Look For?

When you married for the first time, you were probably less mature than you are now. This is especially true if you, like me, were a very young bride the first time around.

Back then, the criteria for finding a soul mate were different than they are today. As a younger woman, your perception of whether a suitor would be a good husband may have revolved around whether he was good-looking, his career plans and educational progress, his family's stability, his sense of humor and how much fun he was in social setting. You based your selection on his *potential*, on what he was likely to *become* as he got older.

Today, you're re-entering the dating world with the benefit of life experience and greater wisdom. It no longer matters so much how cute or how social the guy is if he's kind, considerate, trustworthy and dependable.

Apply the following questions when considering a new fella:

- **Was he raised in a Christian home, with a good example of how to be a husband? Does he love Jesus? Does he lead you to the Lord or draw you away from your faith?** *This is the most important criteria in my book. You can't settle down with a guy who isn't a Christian without major issues arising. You need a man who causes your faith to grow and does his best to model Christ's love to you. It will never work if you're spiritually mismatched.*

- **Is he financially secure?** *You don't want to get tangled up with a guy who's looking to freeload. Some deadbeat men are looking for a "sign-if-I-can't other," one who will "sign if I can't" for a loan. Don't fall for it! Always date men on financial footing equal to or better than yours. As one friend recently said of her second date with her now-second husband, "He started talking about his 800 credit score, and—oh my—I got all hot and bothered! There's nothing sexier than a man with good credit!" You'll avoid a lot of stress if you choose a man who knows how to manage his affairs over one who doesn't. The guys who were wallflowers in high school are often the guys running the world later in life. Give the smart, responsible guy a chance!*

- **How's his work ethic?** *If a guy can't keep a steady job or switches careers regularly, there's usually a reason for that. Run the other way.*

- **Does he have a criminal history?** *Upon request, I often run background searches on my divorce clients' gentleman callers to give the* *all-clear before the relationship becomes serious. It's a good practice; a guy can seem perfect but have a really seedy past, and you need to know that going in.*

- ❖ **Is he good to his own children?** *If he hasn't kept his child support current or seen his children on a consistent basis, that's often a sign of poor character.*
- ❖ **How does he treat his mother?** *A man who mistreats his mother is not a good man. If he loves his mama well, he will probably love you well. But be careful—you don't want some codependent mama's boy or an overinvolved mother-in-law. What you want is for him to have a healthy relationship with his mom, and for his mom not to overstep boundaries and meddle in your relationship.*
- ❖ **Does he get along with his siblings?** *Family discord can often be a red flag. If his siblings don't like him or none of them are close, there's usually a reason and a whole history that you need to understand before joining the family.*
- ❖ **Does he use illegal drugs? Does he drink too much?** *If he uses illegal drugs or abuses alcohol, it's a recipe for disaster. It's especially problematic if you have children, for your ex will have valid concerns about the children's safety and perhaps even grounds to change custody or restrict your parenting time if you bring this kind of guy into your home.*
- ❖ **Does he have anger issues?** *If he rages at his kids or is easily angered at his co-workers, family and friends over seemingly minor matters, this usually means you could be the next target, and you shouldn't hang around waiting for him to turn on you. If he is quick-tempered and shows you that part of himself during the courtship phase when things are supposed to be peachy, this is a warning sign to stop seeing him.*

❖ **Does he have a history of infidelity?** *If so, you're unlikely to change him, no matter his other excellent qualities. You're setting yourself up for heartache. Guard your heart and get away, Dear Friend. There are plenty of men in the world who deserve your attention and don't cheat.*

❖ **Are you considering his traits more than his labels?** *Gretchen Baskerfield, wise author of* The Life-Saving Divorce *which I commend to your reading, wrote that only traits matter when dating, not labels. Gretchen then listed multiple labels like "Pastor," "Widower," "Police Officer," "Dog Lover," "Father," and "Military Officer" which are not guarantees of character. When selecting men to date, you should instead be looking for traits—things like whether he's kind, patient, willing to discuss issues, fair-minded, and self-controlled—which reveal a man's true character.*[5]

Red Flags to Avoid

You can waste a lot of time dating the wrong men. Once you see a guy isn't going to be someone you can be with long term, cut him loose and cut your losses. You should never date someone you know you can't marry. The longer he lingers, the harder it will be to shake him, and you shouldn't date anyone too long after it's clear you'd never want to marry him. The right guy could be out there while you waste good time on this one! Be wise.

Here are a few red flags to avoid:

1. **If there's no peace in the relationship, he's not for you.** I see in my practice many ladies who are naturally drawn to the excitement of a challenge. They run toward (and seem to feed on) relationship drama. But Friend, the stress of that drama

---

[5] Baskerville, Gretchen. *The Life-Saving Divorce* Facebook page, January 24, 2022.

will send you to an early grave. We're told again and again in Scripture that God is love, that our God is a God of peace. So, if we're looking for love, and God *is* both love and peace, it follows that enriching, godly romantic love will manifest in a way that's peaceful, not chaotic or anxiety-ridden. The right guy will lower your blood pressure, calm you down, not keep you in turmoil. Run away if he makes you anxious, keeps you guessing about where you stand with him, or makes you feel unsettled.

2. **If he draws you away from your faith and values, he's not the one.** When I got to the University of Georgia after having been sheltered from the partying element all my life, all that freedom was intoxicating, and I had so much fun dating a really rebellious frat boy freshman year. He was cute, buck wild and so much FUN. Little ole' Southern Baptist me was drawn into the party scene for the first time of my life, and I loved every minute of it for the short time it lasted. He broke my heart, of course, because I just couldn't hang with the craziness he was into. He put me in several truly dangerous situations... he drove drunker than a skunk through the streets of downtown Athens, took me to parties where I later found out serious drugs were being abused, and got us stranded late at night away from our dorms. Oh, how thankful I am now, looking back on it in middle age, for the good Lord's protection! You may be tempted in your phase of newfound freedom to go and sow some oats, but it just isn't wise. Don't even consider dating a bad boy who'll lead you into sin and peril like that. God would never lead you to a relationship that causes you to stumble in your walk with Him.

3. **If he doesn't share your beliefs, it will never work.** God has told us not to be yoked with unbelievers. No matter how successful he is, no matter how nice he is to your mama, no matter how good your chemistry with him may be, it will never work if he doesn't know your Jesus. And you should never allow yourself to choose a life partner who may cause you to doubt or fall away from your faith. Period.

4. **If he doesn't appreciate you, run.** If you're the one chasing connection with him all the time while he ignores or doesn't appreciate you, you'll never be fulfilled. Read 1 Corinthians 13's description of what love is. If you are the one putting in all the effort while he throws no reciprocation your way, he's showing you that he's just not that into you. Cut ties and find someone who will value you for the jewel you are! You are God's precious daughter. Some other lucky fella is sure to recognize it.

Don't Be Afraid to Give New Love a Chance

I'm a clumsy, messy person. I bump into things like doorways and cabinets on a regular basis, completely sober. My car is always cluttered with stuff for the kids' ballgames, client files, hand sanitizer, spare clothes for spray tan day (I go twice a week, religiously). I'm alright with clean clothes remaining draped on a bedroom chair for days until I can get around to hanging them up. I'm a messy cook (when I cook), and I don't always notice when I've left drops of liquid or crumbs on the floor. That stuff just doesn't register with me; I suppose my mind is always on work or my kids instead. Call it my tragic flaw.

During my first marriage, these little annoying things would irritate my husband so much. He would always let me know it if I didn't make a recipe correctly, and Katie bar the door if I happened to put his Dri-fit bike shorts in the dryer by mistake. Little—and, in all fairness, understandable—irritations, created by me. Tension creators.

I admittedly wasn't (and still am not) good at certain things, and he had every reason to be annoyed with me. But our inability to *talk* about it in a healthy way was the beginning of our end. A person who doesn't feel loved and appreciated and another person who is constantly annoyed by the things the first person does, do not a happy marriage make, and this discord leads to bigger, more insurmountable issues. He just needed someone less like me, someone who annoyed him less, I suppose, and that's okay. It wasn't all his fault or all mine—it was just a mismatch from the start, but my feelings just seemed to be hurt all the time back then. I walked around in a constant state of heightened alert and tension, feeling altogether "less than" other women. Questioning my worth. Always wondering if he really loved me. Positively sure he would leave me eventually.

If your ex-husband was harsh or unforgiving with you, you can expect this PTSD sort of impulse to persist in your future relationships. You're healing from trauma, and you will continue to heal for some time. But, Dear Sister, do not make the mistake of assuming all men are like your ex.

There are good, kind men out there looking for connection and compatible with you. Men who can be trusted with your heart. Men who will live to love you, to shelter and protect you. To support you in bad days and encourage you to pursue your dreams. To love you like Christ loves the Church.

I'm all the time making messes and foolish household mistakes to this day—some things never change, I suppose. And for the first few years of my second marriage, I still would find myself tensing up and preparing for the comments I just knew were coming.

But you know what? They never have, not one single time.

Instead of harshness and judgment, I now get laughter and understanding, and he helps me fix the problem. My chronic household failures and disorganization—much to my amazement and comfort—seem to amuse him, to endear me to him even more rather than annoy him. The longer I live with my Jefferson, my True North, in this atmosphere of compassion and acceptance, my PTSD response rears its ugly head less and less.

There are well-raised men out there who are capable of loving you well, Dear Friend. Men who will never make you question your standing with them. God may be preparing him for you right now. He's not your ex. Give him a chance to show you, and don't assume the worst in your suitors. Be open to love and look for the good. Optimism and positive thinking are much more attractive than insecurity and pessimism! If you're feeling those things as you begin your post-divorce dating life, oh-for-the-love, don't let it show!

Your Ex and Kids Could Try to Ruin It

When you're blessed with new love, don't be surprised if your ex tries to interfere and sabotage every bit of it. Maybe he'll be unavailable to have the kids on his parenting time days because he knows you've got plans with the new beau. Or perhaps he'll even contact your fella directly or through other people to say negative things about you in hopes of running him off. Worse, he might say awful, dreadful, false things about Prince Charming to your children so that they will give you flak about moving on. Even worse than that, your ex could stalk or harass both you and your new friend to make your new friend literally afraid to date you anymore. A crazy ex can be the bane of your existence.

The worst thing you can do if your ex tries to ruin your new relationship is let him see that it bothers you. Your new love doesn't need to see your ex get a rise out of you, either. Do not stop living or run off a guy who could be the perfect addition to your life because you can't deal with your ex's efforts to control you. So many women choose not to date at all because of post-divorce manipulation from their exes. He wins if you let him manipulate you into not dating, if you let him steal your hope for a better life, if you deny yourself permission to live your *best* life.

Don't Make It Public Until You Know It's Permanent

Once you find new love after a divorce, you may be tempted to shout it from the social media rooftops. You'll want your new love to meet your family and your children. You'll want other people to see how happy you are and have it get back to your ex.

After years of doing my job in a small town, I can tell it's best to learn to love *in private*. Keep your early dates *private*. Keep your romantic travel plans *private*. The local rumor mill can destroy a new love affair, which is why they shouldn't be allowed access or license to comment. And, for the love, please don't introduce him to your family or your kids until you're certain it's going to be a long-term thing. If you don't use discretion in this, your mama and your children could get attached to the guy just as he's headed out the door, and they could get hurt right alongside you.

Date him, love him, cherish it—in private. If the relationship is that special, it's really only about you and him anyway, and worth shielding from the world, at least for a time. Other people don't need to see it or understand it, so long as you do.

Marin's Story

It had been eight months since the divorce was final on the night I introduced the kids to my now-husband, John. None of them had said a word to him at dinner, and one of them even sent me a rude text while we were at the restaurant to say, "Mom, why did you make us come here tonight?" And then my son was downright rude to John, refusing to shake his hand when John had introduced himself. The kids' dad had told them not to accept any new men I should meet. He had told them all statistics about how stepfathers are often child molesters. The way he had coached my children to sabotage my dating life was nothing short of child abuse.

As I walked John out to his car at the end of the night, with prayers for intervention rising from my heart to the heavens, I just knew my kids had run him off.

But they hadn't.

I looked up at John in the driveway at my house, bracing myself for yet another heartbreak, thankful for the darkness and hoping he couldn't see the tears welling in my eyes. But he didn't break up with me. Instead, he took my elbows in his hands, grinned big and said, "Aw, baby, they're just being kids. They'll come around." I fell more in love with him than ever before in that moment. He wasn't fazed one bit.

The kids eventually warmed up to him and now, six years later, they've come to love him as I do. He's been such a stabilizing force for their lives, an example of how a husband should treat his wife that they'd never experienced before. When their dad has let them down, John has stepped in to encourage and support them, but he hasn't overstepped his bounds one time. He isn't trying to be anyone's father; he just wants to love us.

Oh, the desperation wrapped up in all of this! To be madly in love and hoping it all works with your children, too, is to be ultra-vulnerable. But the Lord works it all together for your good if you love Him and are called according to his purpose, and *no one*—not even your children (or your ex working through your children)—can ruin the right relationship if it's meant to be. And the guy who's been sent from the Lord to join your crazy life won't let anything ruin it. He'll say and do the things that reassure you things are okay, again and again, even when you fear the worst, and he'll wait patiently for your kids to warm up to him, even if it takes a while.

Leave it with the Lord, and don't push relationships on anyone involved. Relationships have to form and grow organically, and you can't force them.

Oh, praise Him for His promise of the new day to come! May we all trade in our ashes for a beautiful future, trade our despair for praise, and display His splendor through His righteous work in all of us. Stay strong and keep moving forward! With each day that passes, you are closer to that brighter day that's coming . . . and don't forget to invite your lawyer to the wedding! People always forget about us. 😉

Questions for Reflection

1. Are you holding onto the past? Remember Lot's wife. What can you do to get over your ex and stop longing for what you once had? Remind yourself of the pain of that relationship and the reasons it needed to end. From what dangerous or harmful thing was God shielding you by allowing your marriage to end?
2. Since you began dating earlier in your life, have you ever been single, i.e., without a boyfriend or husband? Are you someone who feels more comfortable as part of a couple, or are you good on your own?
3. Do you believe you are already whole *without* a man in your life? Make a list of the gifts God has given you that any guy would be overjoyed to have in his wife.
4. What is Proverbs 18:22 tells us that the man who finds a wife finds a treasure, and he receives favor from the LORD. Do you believe it? Do you believe you can be a blessing to a second husband and bring him God's favor? Remind yourself of this truth when you're feeling insecure about getting back into the dating world.
5. Consider the following verses, asking God to be at work in your life, making known His plans for you:

Psalm 147:3
Isaiah 31:3
Joel 2:25
Psalm 30:5
Psalm 37:4
Psalm 126:5

Resources

Attached: The New Science of Adult Attachment and How It Can Help You Find—and Keep—Love—Amir Levine, M.D. & Rachel S.F. Heller, M.A.

The Road Less Traveled—M. Scott Peck

What If It's Wonderful?—Nicole Zasowski

Any novel by Patti Callahan Henry

Heart of Dating Podcast

The Godly Dating 101 Podcast

Chapter Soundtrack

"I Prayed for You"—Matt Stell

"In Your Eyes"—Peter Gabriel

"Heart Like a Truck"—Lainey Wilson

"Same Old Lang Syne"—Dan Fogelberg

"Shot in the Dark"—John Mayer

"Oceans (Where Feet May Fail)"—Hillsong UNITED

"She Won't Be Lonely Long"—Clay Walker

"The Red Strokes"—Garth Brooks

"Goodbye in Her Eyes"—Zac Brown Band

"Thank God"—Kane Brown and Katelyn Brown

"It's All Coming Back to Me Now"—Celine Dion

"Could You Be Loved"—Bob Marley

"Love On the Weekend"—John Mayer

8

Graceful Family Blending

"You'll never be a step-anything."
—Linda Owens, on the day she married my dad

Blended Families are Special

Divorce brings a time of major transition for the children, and introducing new stepparents and stepsiblings brings new challenges. But once the dust settles, a blended family can bless all its members by providing a larger support system, providing children with additional parental resources and role models and exposure to a wider range of experiences, extended family contacts, and opportunities that would otherwise have been unavailable.

It's sometimes difficult for some women to watch their ex-husbands remarry, and there's a tendency to be territorial and resist the input of the new woman regarding parenting matters. But once the initial shock of your ex moving on passes and the dust settles, folks often see the blessings in a stepparent's involvement. What a blessing when stepmom steps in to provide a much-needed, neutral voice of reason, encouraging your hot-headed ex to be calm and fair in his dealings with you! A level-headed stepmother, even if she isn't your favorite person in the world, can be sometimes make an excellent coparent.

Do not be threatened by the new woman. First of all, you should start praying for her now, as she's the current version of you in your ex's life, and tigers don't change their stripes. She's likely enduring what you did when you were with him, so be thankful he's someone else's problem now. Second, she's never going to be your children's mama, and she probably doesn't want to be. If you find yourself feeling jealous of her, remember Lot's wife, and don't allow yourself to look back with longing. Instead, focus on all the ways your children will benefit from having someone new to love them, and the ways she will enrich their childhood. It's about the children now, not you. And, hard as it may be, try to put your hurt feelings aside and give her the benefit of the doubt if something she does or says rubs you the wrong way. It is entirely possible that she truly means you no harm, and you'll be really embarrassed picking fights with her over things that turn out to be small. You must carefully choose your battles, if you choose to battle her at all.

Stepparenting

There's also the possibility that you'll end up with a guy with children from his prior life, so you should start thinking now about how you'll handle the role of stepmother to those children, how you'll introduce the New Mr. Wonderful to your kids, and how you'll help all the kids blend with each other.

In my years of advising parties in post-divorce custody modifications, I've picked up some tidbits of wisdom for stepparents. Here are the top five things stepparents should keep in mind for optimal family blending results:

1. **Stay in your lane.** Recognize the mother's role is paramount to yours and let her know you're no threat to her position, early and often.

2. **Encourage the children to love their mom, and don't let the father alienate the children from her.** Too many coparenting fathers get satisfaction from trying to replace their children's mother with another woman. If this happens to you, remind him and the children that their mother cannot be replaced, and that you're not interested in alienating children from a loving parent.
3. **Don't administer corporal punishment.** It's not your job to spank anyone else's kids, and you can set yourself up for a report to child protection agencies if you do it. Again, stay in your lane.
4. **Encourage the children to show their mother respect.** A stepparent should never badmouth a child's parent in the child's presence or allow that child to speak ill of their parent in the stepparent's presence. The children will respect and love you more if you show you're a person who respects others.
5. **Stay out of coparenting discussions unless you're invited to participate.** You may love these stepchildren and have a strong opinion about what needs to happen in their lives. But you're not their parent, and you have no business interfering unless they ask your opinion. If asked to participate, do your best to be a calm voice of reason instead of stirring the pot. The goal ought to be a peaceful resolution that benefits the children.

All of these same ideas apply to your new fella, too. By insulating him from conflicts with your ex, you can shield him from the stress of it, and also guard against him feeling the need to overstep his boundaries with your children in order to be a shield for you.

Introducing a New Stepparent

I've been a stepchild, and I've counseled hundreds of blended families through all sorts of family dynamics impacting their custody cases over the years. Incorporating a stepparent in the lives of your children can be tricky and create new legal issues that didn't exist before. It's best to head off these issues before they arise to prevent new, expensive, tumultuous family court battles.

As with any other human relationship, you can't force it! Bonds form organically and over time, so try to be patient while everyone around you sorts it out. Your new husband and your children will have their own relationship, in their own way, and the amount of time necessary to get it established could vary from child to child.

A University of Minnesota study[6] found that methods for seamless introduction of a stepparent to a child vary based on the age of the child. The study found the following, based on the age of the child involved:

- Children ages two to five years take more time to process the finality of their family breakup and often still hold out hope that Mommy and Daddy will still reconcile, and they may think they did something to cause the breakup. It's important to let them know it's okay to love their stepparent, and that loving the stepparent doesn't replace or cancel the child's love for you, and that it's okay to be a part of and love two families.
- Elementary school children up ten years old may also feel guilty over the divorce, and these feelings can manifest in poor performance in school or a lack of interest in age-appropriate activities. Kids this age tend to feel life is out of control, so the

---

6   https://extension.umn.edu/divorce-and-other-family-transitions/how-age-affects-childrens-adjustment-stepfamilies

experts recommend giving them a little more input into personal decisions like what clothes they wear, choice of hairstyles, and bedroom décor (while still maintaining basic standards). When a parent remarries with elementary-age children, it ends any illusion of the child's parents reconciling, and the child may regress and grieve the divorce all over again.

- Preteens ages 11–12 tend to pull away from their families and test the boundaries. This is the time, experts warn, when the potential for conflict increases in blended families as children resent and resist the stepparent's authority in the home and blame the stepparent for all the family's problems. Parents and stepparents in this situation must remember to help children think through the consequences of their actions to foster better decision-making, rather than trying to make decisions for them. By giving preteens safe options to consider, all of which being acceptable to you, they begin to feel empowered to exert independence in decision making and, thus, act out less.
- Teenagers from ages 13–18 are becoming more aware of their own sexuality, but they often see their parents as nonsexual and, thus, become uncomfortable with a parent's remarriage and shows of affection with a new spouse. With remarriage, a child this age may lose some of their responsibilities—like caring for younger siblings or having a greater say in matters of household management—as the new spouse assumes those roles. If this is your scenario, it's important to keep communication open with your teen to ensure they know you still love and value them and try to keep giving them roles of importance in the home if that seems to be something they enjoyed. And if your teenager wants to spend more time with your ex just after your remarriage, let them, so long as your

coparent is safe. They're at an age where they will appreciate and respect you more for respecting their need for a little space and autonomy in small matters. If you resist their wishes in this regard, it could backfire, and they could reject you entirely for a time because "you're treating them like a baby." I've seen it happen many times.

No matter the age of the child, adjusting to a blended family is always a time of transition. Give everyone grace as they adjust to the new normal.

How a Prenuptial Agreement Can Keep Your Next Marriage Together

According to a 2023 Forbes study[7] on divorce, thirty-seven percent of divorcees surveyed noted "financial disagreements" as a major cause of the divorce, while another fifty-eight percent cited "too much conflict and arguing" as a major cause.

You can avoid this kind of discord by laying out all your financial expectations, before you marry, in a prenuptial agreement.

A good prenuptial agreement addresses not only how assets and debts will be divided (and how alimony will be awarded, if at all) should the marriage end in divorce, but also how you will manage the finances as a married couple. A prenuptial agreement often protects each party's premarital property and earnings/wealth accumulation during the marriage from being lost in the event of divorce, as well.

There is no reason to give up your financial independence just because you've remarried. A new husband will respect you for having—and managing—your own money, and you will likewise respect him for his financial independence. For this reason, I usually recommend remarrying

---

7   https://www.forbes.com/advisor/legal/divorce/divorce-statistics/ (citing data from the National Library of Medicine).

parties keep their bank accounts separate for general operating purposes so there are no arguments over how anyone spends their disposable income, and that Party One pay the other a set amount each month, ideally via direct deposit on the first day of each month, to contribute to the household bills Party 2 actually pays; this limits the potential for anyone ever to feel the other party isn't pulling their weight.

I often recommend parties to second marriages have a joint bank account to which each party transfers a certain amount monthly for date nights, the couple's vacations, gifts from the couple to third party relatives, and other things the parties may want to buy together. This gives the couple a fun little joint venture to enjoy together, free of the pressure to spend beyond their means on trips and other luxuries they can't afford which, we all know, can lead to financial stress and unnecessary strife.

The prenuptial agreement is the ideal place to memorialize not only this bank account management plan but also other expectations for the marriage like estate planning (to preserve assets for your children) and how household finances will be managed, *before* the marriage occurs. It can be a difficult conversation to have, but better to have it before the wedding to avoid marital issues later. If both parties know what to expect financially and with the running of the household, they will argue less. Some say prenuptial agreements are unromantic. To me, they just make good common sense, exposes any impure motivations for marrying, and keep marriages running smoothly.

Living with a guy without marrying him can bring its own legal issues. If you choose to do this, consider forming a cohabitation agreement before you move in together. A cohabitation agreement can address the same issues a prenup does, along with other things like the plan for one party to move out of the home if the parties should break up, so that a formal eviction or other dispossessory action won't be needed.

Questions for Reflection

1. If you worry about your children having to adjust to a new stepmom, what things worry you most? Are the worries truly tied to their needs, or are they personal to you? Are you ready to co-parent with your ex and any new love in his life, or does the very thought of it make you cringe?
1. What are your children's unique needs and qualities to be taken into consideration before introducing a new stepfather in your home?
1. How easily does each child adapt to big changes? How are they adapting just to your separation from their father so far? What can you learn from what's happened so far to help you guide them through other life changes as they come after your divorce?
1. How can you have age-appropriate discussions with each of your children to help them adjust to new love interests in their parents' lives?
1. Have you considered a prenuptial agreement? If not, why not?

Resources

Coparenting Works!—Tammy Daughtry

Stepmom Magazine

The Five Love Languages of Teenagers—Gary Chapman

101 Tips for the Smart Stepmom—Laura Petherbridge

Before You Remarry: A Guide to Successful Remarriage—H. Norman Wright

But I'm Not a Wicked Stepmother!—Kathi Lipp and Carol Boley

The Smart Stepdad—Ron Deal

The Smart Stepfamily—Ron Deal

Chapter Soundtrack

"Next Girl"—Carly Pearce

"Landslide"—Fleetwood Mac

"A Face to Call Home"—John Mayer

9

There's Hope for Us All

Delight yourself in the Lord, *and he will give you the desires of your heart.*
—Psalm 37:4

Blessed is she who has believed that the Lord would fulfill his promises to her.
—Luke 1:45

Oh, Friend. I hope by now you're as convinced as I am that there is a good plan for your life and every reason to have hope for a bright future after your divorce.

If you read my first book, you know a little of my story and how my second husband came out of nowhere, knocked me off my feet and transformed my life in every way. I never dreamed it would happen to me, but God's plan was, of course, perfect, as usual. I'm living proof miracles still happen. Jefferson Howell was, is, and will forever be the carrier of God's message to my heart that I am worth loving and that God wants to give us the desires of our hearts, even when we don't even know what that looks like.

But let's be clear. Happiness and fulfilment don't always come in the form of a new romantic love. Sometimes, they come in the form of God teaching you to love and accept *yourself*. You. Special, unique, capable, beautiful *you*. His beloved daughter.

I could write a hundred stories about the clients I've seen go on after divorce to meet their true soul mates. And I could probably write *two* hundred stories of women who—by finding themselves, their peace, and their unique purpose—impact the world in amazing ways after leaving abusive or toxic marriages, *without a new man.*

Over the years, I've observed that the happiest divorced people are those who know the importance of connecting with other people in a meaningful way. God put us on earth to love one another, to serve one another, to take care of one another's needs. What I've seen is when people look for ways to help and connect with other people, their souls are content. God gave you special, you-specific gifts to be used in the world for His glory. Use them. Connect. Love people. Hug them. Tell them you love them. Show your children how to love.

Show your warmth. Give compliments freely. Look for ways to brighten days. Throw away the fear. Embrace the future. Believe good things are possible. Reconnect with your unjaded twenty-year-old self. Be open to new experiences. Use your gifts and volunteer your time. Use your pain to help those with the same struggles. Bear their burdens and let them help you bear yours. Show your children how to live in community. It's what life is really all about.

You have great value. Go contribute something meaningful! When you give of yourself, it's amazing how much life enrichment you get back. And when you find fulfillment as a single person, that's usually when you meet some other single someone—maybe a really cute single someone—doing the same things. All in God's timing.

God cares about the small details of our lives. He knows the longings of our hearts. He is faithful and He is with you. He wants to bless you—with new relationships, experiences, fun times, greater confidence,

There's Hope for Us All | 83

a renewed sense of purpose. My prayer is that your heart be fully healed, that you will feel God's love for you in your depth of your spirit, and that you will lean into His goodness and plan for you, knowing that nothing is impossible with God. Through the words of these pages, I hope you can feel my love and my prayers for your sweet heart. I'm standing and believing in the name of Jesus that you will be blessed.

If you're starting over after your divorce, be proud of yourself for pushing through and not allowing it to break you. You've done a very hard thing! Get excited, girl! You're about to embark on a grand adventure! God is doing a sacred work in you. Let Him transform you into the person He calls you to be and listen for His voice as you walk out your days.

I'll be right here rooting for you. ♥

xo, BSH

Questions for Reflection

1. What do you want your life to look like in one year? Two years? Five years?
2. What can you do to invest in the hearts and lives of others?
3. What gifts do you have to share with the world around you?
4. What do you want people to say about you after you're gone? What legacy do you want to leave behind?
5. What is the deepest desire of your heart? Find your delight in the Lord and pray that these desires will be fulfilled. I'll be praying with you. ♥

Chapter Soundtrack

"Bless the Broken Road"—Rascal Flatts

"Cowboy Take Me Away"—The Chicks

"Perfect"—Ed Sheeran

"Slide"—Goo Goo Dolls

"High On You"—Survivor

"She's In Love"—Mark Wills

"Power of Two"—Indigo Girls

"I See It Now"—Tracy Lawrence

"Love Will Come to You"—Indigo Girls

"Safe in the Arms of Love"—Martina McBride

"Everything Has Changed"—Ed Sheeran & Taylor Swift

"Coming Around Again"—Carly Simon

"Taking You Home"—Don Henley

"Last Train Home"—John Mayer

"Hanging By a Moment"—Lifehouse

"Goodness of God"—The Worship Initiative, Bethany Barnard

Acknowledgments

This labor of love was inspired by my children and sweet Jefferson. I live each day to make all of you proud, and I love you more than words can say.

The idea for writing my books came to me around a dinner table with new friends at Cape Santa Maria, a sacred place so dear to Jefferson and me, an isolated utopia of warmth, kindness, love and peace, precious stray cats, conch fritters and pineapple rum drinks, which came to be the place I've written some of my favorite chapters—both of my life and of this book. I first fell in love with Jefferson there, and I fall more in love with him each time we go. Let yourself go, and you're sure to go back.

I would not have been able to pull off this work without the love and support of my family and friends. Mom and Daddy, you have always made me know how loved I was, and it's been that foundation that gave me the courage to step out and share my thoughts so vulnerably. You are the best parents any kid ever had.

To my family from the farm on Dias Road and throughout Baker County, I wouldn't be me without all of you. Farm love, long talks on hay bales, Pa Heard's house, late-night manicures, Chase from Lolly, chip dip from a yellow Tupperware, and 24-hour coffee forever!

To Aunt Sheila and Aunt Donna, it was so great being the only girl in the sea of boy cousins. Thank you for always being so kind to me, and for supporting my dad while also remaining friendly with my mother after their divorce. You showed me this kind of grace is possible. Pop and Mama Chris raised y'all right.

To my step-people from Bainbridge, thank you for never treating me like a "step-anything." I loved Linda so much, and I love you all.

To Sutton Howell Fyfe, your positivity and kindness in all things inspire me. I always wanted a sister, and you are the perfect one. God gave me a tremendous gift when He gave you, your parents, and Will to me.

Special thanks to Nicole, Leigh Ann and Claley for putting up with me at the office every day. You are the backbone of my practice, and you bless our clients. There's no way I could do this job without you!

To the Smart Girls Travel Club who taught me to embrace adventure and to step out of my comfort zone, time with each of you is life-giving. Now that my first two books are done, let's plan our next trip!

To Susan, Julie, Cindy, Kristin, Caroline, Cheryl, Allison, Kelly, Deb, Nadia, Janna, Jaci, Tricia, Leah, Laura, Jennifer, Ursula, April, Sophie, Cheryl, Leigh, my church family and praise team, Diane Allen and Tracy Bane, who got me through my divorce and showed me life could be good again. You don't even know how much you've blessed my heart with your kind words, reassurance, and encouragement to keep going.

To Christine Lamb, Rebecca McKemie, Jennifer D., Jennifer B., and the ladies of Ally B Boutique, Nailsville and Thomasville Zoom Tan, all of whom who helped me get my groove back. You made it a little less stressful to start dating again after 20 years. 😌

I also thank fellow authors Amy Smith Hobbs and Nadia Watts, book coaches Michelle Melton Cox and Suzette Mullen, and copyright/trademark attorney Angie Avard Turner for all your helpful insight. You are all phenomenal, fierce women I want to be more like.

To Tonya Taylor Brown, Chris Pugh and my mom, who helped me bring my living and work spaces to life with color, art and paint. You are masters of design, painting and art. Thank you for helping create new spaces for new, happy memories and meaningful work.

I especially thank you, my clients, for I would have no wisdom to share if you hadn't allowed me to join you on your legal and personal journeys. I was thinking of you—and speaking to you—with every page of this work. I hope I've given you some useful food for thought.

Above all, I praise and thank my Jesus for loving me, being ever so near in all of the low places of my life, for touching my heart, for giving me hope and courage to offer this work to the world, and for making himself real to me. He has never forsaken me or left me for a second, and he'll never forsake you, either. I can't wait to get to Heaven to meet him face to face.

About the Author

Bree Sullivan-Howell, J.D., with her impeccable record of academic achievements and commitment to justice, has distinguished herself as a top divorce lawyer over her twenty-year career. After graduating with a perfect GPA from the University of Georgia, and then from Mercer University School of Law with honors, Bree quickly established herself as a force in family law. Beyond the courtroom, Bree is an unwavering advocate for domestic abuse survivors and children. Bree's combination of vast legal expertise and profound personal experiences made her debut book, *Crush Your Divorce & Keep Your Faith,* and now this follow-up book, essential guides of encouragement and empowerment for Christian women walking through the harsh reality of divorce. A devoted wife to the love of her life, Jefferson, and loving mother of three almost-grown children, Bree is living proof that life goes on after divorce, and that God's plans for us are always good, even when we can't see it yet. Her passion is to help people crush the hold divorce has over their lives with grace, integrity and grit, and to give them hope for the brighter day to come.

Let's connect!

Instagram: @lawyerbree || @crushyourdivorce

Facebook: Sullivan Law Firm

Linked In: Bree Sullivan-Howell, J.D.

www.sullivan-firm.com || www.crushyourdivorce.com

#crushyourdivorce® || Crush Your Divorce®

Made in the USA
Middletown, DE
16 December 2024